Devil
in the
Details

Kevin J. Kennedy

iUniverse, Inc.
Bloomington

Devil in the Details

iUniverse books may be ordered through booksellers or by contacting:

iUniverse
1663 Liberty Drive
Bloomington, IN 47403
www.iuniverse.com
1-800-Authors (1-800-288-4677)

ISBN: 978-1-4759-2014-7 (sc)
ISBN: 978-1-4759-2015-4 (hc)
ISBN: 978-1-4759-2016-1 (e)

Library of Congress Control Number: 2012907807

Printed in the United States of America

iUniverse rev. date: 4/26/2013

One man with courage makes a majority.

—Andrew Jackson

Contents

Foreword

The night was young, but the party was already in full, riotous swing. Earlier that day, our skiers had captured the first World Cup win by a US team on US soil. A restaurant roped off its second floor for our party, and people flew in from around the world to celebrate with us. Congratulatory phone calls, emails, and champagne toasts poured in nonstop from friends and competitors alike.

As the team's coach, I could have been cheering the loudest and longest of anyone, and I certainly did my share of celebrating that night. But after a while, I slipped out the back, went home, and sat alone in my living room in the dark. What I felt more than anything else was a paralyzing fear. We were on the world's radar now. How was I going to lead these young skiers to their next victory, their next milestone? More important, how was I going to help them become not just stars but true athletes, and from there help them to coalesce into a powerful, cohesive team? I had no idea, but I did know two things: it was going to take more courage and motivation than I'd ever had to muster in my life, and I couldn't do it alone.

I needed to surround myself with people—from the trainers to the medical technicians to the assistant coaches—who were willing and able to take the same kinds of risks I was taking, to live out on the limb with me. There wouldn't be any easy formulas; every race would be different, and we on the management team would need athletes'-level stamina in order to develop a winning system and then dig into the details of each situation to figure out what it would take to win one particular race at a time, time after time.

As Kevin Kennedy explains in *Devil in the Details*, this is exactly what it takes to succeed as a business leader. In this book, he invites you to step into a variety of real-world situations to discover how you would approach specific business problems. You'll also see what other people did, and whether their choices led to success or failure.

The stories in this book are authentic. The author lived through each and every one of them, and in my nearly twenty years as a leadership coach, I have seen some of the world's most influential executives get tied up over exactly the same problems you will find described in these pages, sometimes agonizing over them for months. Anyone who has tried to lead an organization of any size understands that human beings are naturally drawn to drama; teams can be exhausting to work with, and even the best leaders sometimes wonder where they will find the courage and motivation to drive forward. As Kevin correctly observes, the differentiating factor is the leader's ability to shed what he calls "our own prison of perspectives," the set of assumptions we all develop based on our personal experiences. Nothing is more dangerous for a leader than trying to live in a comfortable "zone of safety." The most successful athletes and executives understand not only what they know and what has helped them succeed in the past, but also what they *don't* know. They study the unique details of every situation to help them decide how to move forward.

When people find out who some of my leadership coaching clients are, they often ask me, "What traits do the most successful Olympic athletes and the most successful business leaders have in common?" I understand their curiosity; very few people are ever allowed into the coveted Olympic inner circle. We watch these athletes on television every four years, we get caught up in the excitement, and it all looks pretty glamorous. But if you had the privilege to be in this circle, what you'd really see is a ferocious and very *un*glamorous attention to the details.

You'd also see tremendous courage, and by that, I don't mean athletic courage so much as athletes' courage to assess themselves and others critically and without bias. These people continually push themselves in pursuit of their idea of perfection. One of the most talented Olympic athletes I ever worked with quit the sport after several spectacular years (while still in his prime), because he decided that what he really wanted was to be a multimillionaire before he was forty. Whether or not you find his choice morally appealing, the fact is that today he is thirty-seven years old and a millionaire several times over, and he remains one of the most honestly self-aware individuals I've ever known. Here's another example: After that dark night of the soul in my living room, I realized that some of the people I worked the most closely with, a couple of whom were my best friends, weren't going to be up to the challenge of what we had to do to take the team to the next level. So I replaced them. I fired ten coaches and dozens of athletes in ten years, handpicking and hand-building my teams. I've been described as having a take-no-prisoners attitude, and I can't argue with the assessment.

Another question I'm frequently asked is, "How does this CEO or that CEO do it?" My answer is usually, "How much time do you have?" I don't intend to be sarcastic, but I do want to make the point that successful leadership is complex, situational, and tough. Sure, there are how-to business books that can make the reader feel more successful simply by reading the text cover to cover, but they have no impact on behavior or results in the real world. In contrast, Kevin offers unique and practical insights that make this book much more than a feel-good nightstand read. It does one of the best jobs of distilling and explaining leadership that I have ever seen. If you are willing to put in a bit of mental effort, this book will reward you with a unique, challenging, and proven perspective that you can put into practice immediately.

In this book and in his own career, Kevin expects leaders to think for themselves. As you read, you will be challenged to reflect honestly on your true goals and on how committed you are to achieving them. Anyone who has successfully led world-class organizations, either in business or sports, has often asked in moments of self-doubt, "What do I do now?" This book goes a long way toward helping you find the answers, often by inspiring you to look within yourself.

After reading this book, expect to walk away asking yourself three critical questions: (1) Do I have or can I muster the courage to assess the reality and totality of what I must do to lead successfully? (2) Do I have a process for moving forward that will drive improvement, execution, and discovery? (3) Do I have the team that possesses the specialized mentality and intrinsic passion for getting the details right?

There is no shortage of books that lay out a supposed path to leadership success. What sets this book apart is that it doesn't just give you a blueprint for success; it provides a lens to look through—a way of thinking about the challenges you confront every day—and a set of tools to help you apply these insights in your day-to-day professional life. Whether you're a senior functional expert who wants to be a better team leader or a middle manager looking to branch out or move up, you're about to learn a winning philosophy that has worked for top executives and Olympic athletes alike.

★★★★

Tom Steitz is Founding Partner and CEO of 3 PEAKS Leadership, one of the world's leading leadership firms consulting to the senior executives and leadership teams of many FORTUNE 500 companies. Before beginning his executive coaching career in 2000, Tom was Head Coach for the US Olympic Nordic Combined skiing team, appointed after the 1988 Olympics when the United States finished dead last. When he took over, the US team had very little financial support, insufficient athletic talent, and virtually no respect in Europe. Under his leadership, the US Nordic Combined team went on to win its first medal and amass a winning record that has yet to be replicated. Tom was named International Coach of the Year three consecutive times, and the US Olympic Committee and the US Ski Team have called him "the most successful coach ever" in the sport. Tom's list of coaching "firsts" includes: the first World Junior medal and World Junior team medal for the United States; the first World Cup win on US soil for the United States; the first World Cup team podium finish; coaching the first two US athletes to win a World Cup competition in the same year; the first World Championship; and the United States' best Olympic finish to date.

Preface

As you rise through the ranks in your functional specialty or expand into new functions, you'll be challenged to make leadership decisions in areas where you aren't an expert. In those situations, leaders often fall back on conventional wisdom to guide their decisions. The premise of this book is that using conventional wisdom to guide decision making is perilous. Strong leaders seek to make superior decisions by combining situational courage with a passion for process and a bias toward judgments based on insightful details.

Of all the possible factors that could contribute to a leader's effectiveness, why am I convinced that these three—courage, process, and details—hold the key to successful decision making in the vast majority of situations you will face in your career? Because that is what I've seen and experienced over more than four decades, from my early years as a young engineer in the lab to the CEO's office where I sit today, with my name on the door.

Put simply:

- You can only be as good as the *courage* you muster to face reality, whether the decisions you're called upon to make are narrow and tactical or strategic ones affecting your entire company.
- *Process* is what allows you to align people around you and find out what you don't know. Without process, execution can't be predictable or repeatable.

- The *details* make all the difference, whether you're a chef tackling a new recipe, a physician recommending a treatment plan, or a manager trying to understand why a product isn't selling well.

Courage, process, and details animated every leadership success I've ever witnessed or been part of, just as their absence—or the absence of balance among them—animated just about every leadership failure.

In this book, you will enter many business situations and meet the managers who either navigated those situations successfully or failed to do so, leading their teams and their businesses astray. I assure you that I have been both successful and unsuccessful more times than I can count in the course of my career, and my personal experiences live on (sometimes to my embarrassment) in these illustrative stories. There is one personal experience, though, that still has tremendous resonance and power for me many years after the fact. You can judge whether the outcome was a leadership success, a leadership failure, or something in between. What sticks with me is the way courage, process, and details led to a critical decision in a high-stakes leadership challenge.

In September 2003, the JDS Uniphase Corporation (commonly known as JDSU) board of directors asked me to lead the company as chief executive officer. At that time I had been a board member for less than two years, and the company was still feeling the effects of the telecom bust of 2001. JDSU had suffered an 88 percent decline in revenues and a 98 percent decline in market capitalization. Although I knew the markets and core technologies would heal and grow over time, I also knew I couldn't wait it out. The board, the company leadership team, and the shareholders expected swift action. What's more, although virtually every telecom company was struggling at the time, the JDSU drama had a troublesome aspect that was difficult for me to handicap coming into the job. The company was confronted by a shareholder lawsuit, asserted by the attorney general of the State of Connecticut nominally on behalf of a state pension fund that alleged that former JDSU executives had engaged in insider trading and that the company had failed to disclose material information to investors.

When I took the job, I accepted the conventional wisdom that this was one of hundreds of nuisance lawsuits filed in the wake of a bubble bursting, that this too would pass, and that in the worst case, the matter would be settled by the company's insurers within the company's liability insurance.

The lawsuit claimed damages of up to $20 billion at a time when the market capitalization of the company was $3 billion or less. In essence, I am convinced that JDSU was assailed by a state attorney general seeking political capital and that the state of Connecticut was seeking to bankrupt JDSU and position the company and its former executives in a place of dishonor on the front page of the *Wall Street Journal*—a trophy case against corporate corruption.

With the scene set, let's see how this drama played out, paying particular attention to the impact of (1) demonstrating courage; (2) establishing process; and (3) finding insight by examining the details of the situation.

Courage

Together with the board, I as the CEO had to decide between settlement and resting the case in the hands of a jury. The conventional wisdom argued for settlement; fewer than one tenth of 1 percent of such cases go to a jury verdict and almost all settle before that point. Every expert consulted by the board asserted these points over and over. My choice to take the matter to a jury was challenged frequently, beginning immediately and growing in intensity through the weeks and months of the trial. On the day the judge instructed the jury in advance of their deliberations (which happened to be my birthday), the board met once again. I remember the moment well. As the board meeting ended, a consensus of the board members decided that we should send a message to the other side by offering to settle.

This was the first time in the more than five years of this marathon that the majority of the board held a position I was not personally aligned with. I told the board I believed their decision was wrong, and that while I would do as they instructed, they should plan to find a new CEO the following week. Now, I'll admit that I can be pretty stubborn, but that wasn't what made me so strident in this situation. First, I believed we had good facts and a good chance of winning. Second, it was clear to me that the plaintiff wanted to bankrupt the company; if the plaintiff won, the company could opt to go into bankruptcy and likely improve any settlement during this recourse. And third, in the end, our obligation was to do all we could to protect current shareholders.

The renewed level of passion had its impact. The board agreed not to abandon the process we had adopted, but instead to get more data.

Process

I had to accept the stark reality of the situation: First, this drama could bankrupt the company, so we couldn't base our course of action on hope alone. Second, any leader in a high-stakes situation needs to be humble enough to understand that some of his or her past experiences will shed valuable light on the matter at hand and others will be of little value. Our board was a very thoughtful group of business leaders, but they didn't have backgrounds in the legal profession, nor did I. This board had no reason to think I would bring any unique technical insight to this problem.

Our chairman, Marty Kaplan, and our legal team (Chris Dewees, Matt Fawcett, and Andy Pollack) recognized early that there would be some pressure to make decisions quickly, and I was convinced that we needed to adopt the mindset of marathon runners, not sprinters. An intense but dispassionate and nonpartisan process would be the best medicine for keeping the board aligned over a multiyear marathon. We discussed issues, progress, and decisions, first quarterly, then monthly, then weekly, and—during the trial—almost daily. Consistent with good corporate governance practices, we invited external experts to inform the board. These experts included but were not limited to the primary legal team for the defense (Morrison and Foerster), other legal firms for second and third opinions, a professional and highly experienced arbitrator, a renowned former federal judge, the general counsels of other public companies, and so forth.

Details

Every expert who was brought in to assess the case found the facts to be favorable to the company and the individual defendants. The board had done its own review of the facts, and the results were consistent with the third-party assessments. The facts were basically good, and there was no indication of any foul play.

You wouldn't have concluded that from reading the suit, however. It included allegations attributed to nominally confidential witnesses, generally former employees, who were claimed to have smoking gun knowledge of wrongdoing. While the expected number of such depositions might be on the order of ten, plus or minus, the prosecution called more than fifty. Interestingly enough, when their names were disclosed and they were deposed, not one of these witnesses produced any information that led to a smoking gun; in fact, many testified that the allegations attributed to them were not correct, and not one was called by the plaintiff to testify at trial.

If you ever doubt the pervasiveness of conventional wisdom, consider this: Although the facts appeared to be favorable to JDSU, all of our external legal advice recommended that the company settle the case before the jury began deliberation. Remember, there was little precedent to suggest that we could litigate, take the case to trial, and win a favorable jury verdict. Furthermore, for many in the legal community, a settlement is a way for no one to lose (other than perhaps an innocent company and its current shareholders).

Our legal team conducted quite a few mock trials, some lasting one day, others two. That was significant, since the trial was set in the Northern District of California, a jurisdiction known to be somewhat unfavorable to corporate America. The prosecution was betting that the juries would be selected from a demographic in northern California, which they felt would not be sympathetic to a corporation. But the details of the mock trials were revealing. In the one-day mock trials, the jury found in favor of the company, with a slight margin. In the two-day mock trials, the juries found in favor of the company almost 100 percent of the time. In short, the more details the juries learned, the more they based their decisions on the facts rather than on conventional wisdom.

As it turned out, the dynamics we observed in the mock trials played out on the main stage. The judge required the trial jury to answer detailed questions spanning the twenty-four counts charged against the company. Armed with a wealth of details, the jury appeared to share a general perception that the plaintiff was asserting an ideological position, while the defense was focused on demonstrating the facts of the case.

So how did it turn out? The jury found the company and the defendants not liable on all twenty-four counts. This was a landmark outcome, especially when you consider that the company had to win every point in order to win the case. More than five years later, the case became one of fewer than five cases out of 2,150 shareholder lawsuits in the years from 1996 to 2007 that went to a jury trial and was not settled for a sum of money. The integrity of the company and the defendants was reinforced, and the current shareholders were protected from the financial impact of a settlement. The company avoided bankruptcy or any transfer of wealth away from JDSU shareholders.

If this were the script for a movie, it might be all too easy to cast the CEO as a noble and unshakable hero, so firm in his convictions that he is willing to stand—alone, if need be—against the tide of collective opinion. But as you may already have discovered in your career, the kind of oversimplification familiar to moviegoers bears little resemblance to the complex and often messy reality of real-life leadership situations. The truth is that, despite the many favorable facts in this case, I struggled with painful self-doubt for a very long time. Suffice it to say, when just about every expert and nonexpert believes that you are headed down the wrong path, even the firmest self-confidence can be shaken. And as you can see, the experience is still with me.

Courage, Process, and Details

Let me make one more observation, inspired by an event that hit the business press literally as I was writing this book. The board of directors of HP initiated the transition from a single CEO to two board members, one to act as executive chairman and the other to act as CEO. Given that the ousted CEO had been in the job for barely one year and was HP's fifth CEO in less than a decade, public drama surrounded this transition.

Generally speaking, transitions are difficult, whether it's the transition to a new product line, a new business model, or a new CEO. Unlike a seasoned management team, boards as operating bodies do not manage transitions frequently or with the ease that comes from practice. They are often called upon to make sensitive decisions in the glare of the public spotlight, pressured by stress and drama inside the organization. This can be a complex and debilitating process. Reporting on the HP transition, James B. Stewart of the *New York Times* quoted an unnamed board member as saying, "I admit it was highly unusual, but we were just too exhausted from all the infighting." [*New York Times*, "Voting to Hire a Chief Without Meeting Him," Sept. 21, 2011]

I have, however, closely observed an alternative approach to a CEO transition. The process went this way:

- A current board member was established as interim CEO.
- An executive search was conducted.
- Two finalists were identified.
- Both finalists interviewed with all members of the board individually.
- Both finalists participated in separate three-hour sessions with the board as a whole, exploring in detail how they would go about their new role. This step was more about assessing interpersonal dynamics than about gathering information, since it gave the board the opportunity to interact with the candidates as if they were already members of the team.
- A finalist was chosen.
- The interim CEO shadowed the new CEO for four weeks to ensure the integrity of the transition.

Whether at the level of the board or the level of a project team, change attracts drama, and drama can make a leader's job much more difficult. Courage, process, and attention to detail can defuse the drama that comes naturally to human beings and greatly increase the probability of a favorable outcome. Throughout the stories in this book, you will watch the interplay of courage, process, and detail and see for yourself how our cast of characters navigates those situations, for better and for worse. Who will get it right? Who will make things worse? What would you have done? Now let's get started!

Acknowledgments

In many Acknowledgments sections, the author's family comes last, which I suspect is generally how these family members feel while their loved ones are mired in the long process of gestating books like this one. Since my family probably felt the same way, let me put them first here, with deep gratitude for their tolerance, their feedback and suggestions, and their repeated and necessary insistence that I temper my passion for analysis with compassion for the human beings I have written this book for and about. I am especially grateful to my wife, Barb, whom you will read about in these pages. She has taught me much about the courage of everyday heroes. I also thank my children for improving my sense of humor.

My thanks to Mary Moore, an organizational consultant and the coauthor of my first book, *Going the Distance*. Mary helped me frame the initial structure of *Devil in the Details*, giving me a solid and very helpful starting point.

In the early stages of the manuscript, Scott Kriens, Geoffrey Moore, and Sanjay Vaswani generously provided insightful feedback and direction and kept me from wandering off on any number of tangents.

As the book took shape, many people were extremely generous with their time and perspective during a series of midcourse reviews. I would particularly like to acknowledge Mohamad Ali, Ric Andersen, Betsy Atkins, Jake Chacko, Jim Chirico, Pam Craven, John DiLullo, Cary FitzGerald, Steve Fitzgerald, Roger Gaston, Charlie Giancarlo, Joel Hackney, Penny Herscher, Marty Kaplan, Kevin Rollins, the Honorable Greg Slayton, Gary Smith, and Rick Wallace.

My sincere thanks to Tom Steitz for providing the Foreword, as well as for his coaching and inspiration on and off the "field."

As all of these people would tell you, I am an operational leader, not a professional writer. Kit Stinson and David Shaw made my prose livelier and more accessible than it would have been without their expertise. I am deeply grateful. Thanks, too, to Patrick Graziano for his help with the illustrations.

Finally, my heartfelt appreciation and respect go to the many people not named here, people I have worked with and for over the years. They are the raw material for this book, and the characters in the stories. It has been a blessing to solve problems, grow companies, and learn from them.

Introduction

It's human nature to complain. Visit just about any company, whether successful or struggling, and you'll see that for yourself. The villain in the complaint of the day may be the boss, or the company, or simply "them." Most of the time, nobody asks who "they" are. Catharsis feels good, and for many employees, so does blaming someone else.

Unless you happen to be the boss, or the project leader, or an employee at any level who feels personally accountable for the success of the company. Then there's nowhere to run and no one else to blame. The buck, as it's said, stops with you.

If you're a dedicated manager who sincerely wants to be a better leader, you've probably read books on leadership, attended seminars on effective management techniques, maybe even taped some inspiring slogans up on your wall: things like "When the going gets tough, the tough get going," or "Leaders aren't born, they're made." Every morning, you resolve that this day will be a major step forward in your leadership effectiveness. And many evenings, you glumly admit it wasn't.

What's the matter with you? Probably nothing. What's the matter with the way you're trying to rally your team, solve business problems, and drive repeatable successes? Possibly a lot, and to make matters even murkier, you may be looking for answers in the wrong places.

Let's face it: People in business school typically don't study how to identify and correct leadership problems, or if they do, they use abstract exercises built on business cases based on situations that happened to somebody else. As a result, when they get into the workplace and face challenging real-life situations, they have no behavioral reference from their own experience to draw on. Now, I have nothing against business schools; I believe in education. But the most powerful leadership development happens in the trenches in real time.

So where do developing leaders look for guidance? Maybe to that inspiring sticky note tacked up on the wall, or to their own bosses (who may be equally clueless), or to that universal mentor, the online search engine. But sticky notes don't understand the details of the specific situation at hand, and neither does the search engine. The boss may not ask the right questions to help the manager uncover the situational details that will lead to a successful solution. And mentoring is great if you can get it, but very few employers are committed to supporting robust, intelligent mentoring programs that lead to sustained positive results.

So the manager is often left with generic advice and conventional wisdom. Thus feebly armed, the manager retreats to a personal zone of safety, by which I mean a rote way of thinking or behaving that is the manager's natural course of least resistance. Zones of safety offer the comfort of the familiar, but they rarely help managers get to the heart of the issue at hand, let alone find a creative way through it. We'll see a lot of zone-of-safety behavior throughout this book.

The stories you'll find here are drawn from my experiences in computing, software, communications equipment, and other market segments. I have lived through all the stories I tell in this book. As I say to my own leadership team, I wouldn't ask you to do anything I wouldn't do myself.

Some of the stories take the form of fables. In addition to being engaging and accessible, fables have a wonderful way of illustrating the limitations of conventional wisdom and the triumph of counterintuitive thinking. Fables often express polarities, or direct opposites, to establish a meaningful contrast: the slow tortoise versus the speedy hare, or the forceful wind versus the more subtle, distant sun in the story that follows. In business, as in fables, the obvious choice—the conventional wisdom—usually turns out to be wrong. Here's an example:

Aesop's fable "The Wind and the Sun" describes a contest between (yes) the wind and the sun. To determine which was stronger, the sun and wind used their respective powers to remove a young man's cloak as he walked down a road.

The wind blew hard and nearly knocked the traveler down, but the young man just pulled his cloak more tightly around him. The sun, on the other hand, silently and deliberately burned ever hotter. Eventually the heat was so intense that the young man removed his cloak. The sun won, not by bravado or battering force, but through patience and insight into human behavior. The moral for leaders is that either overt force or subtle influence can inspire people to action, but influence is much more likely to produce the desired result.

We live in a world that doesn't wait for leaders to develop over many years, through one experience after another and from one mentor to another. This isn't 1940 or, for that matter, 1990. Today, someone in college may create the next big thing and become a millionaire long before—or instead of—graduation. Or you may be doing something you love, only to have the market find you; the optics explosion in the 1990s, for example, was more about a market finding a technology than the other way around. Today's developing leaders need a lens, a reliable, repeatable way to help them look at the world, understand what they're seeing, and take action.

Fables are a simple kind of lens. This book offers a lens with a few more facets, created from a mix of courage, process, and details. It's designed to help you practice mentally by placing you in a variety of challenging business situations and allowing you to observe how the various characters behave. Ultimately, my goal is to give you some tools and frameworks that en*courage* you to resist the seductive pull of conventional wisdom and zones of safety. By learning to look for the defining details in a situation, you can become adept at designing and executing effective (and often quite simple) solutions, time after time.

Two fundamental personal beliefs anchor this book:

The first is that organizations—like individuals—are living organisms with personalities, cultural behaviors, intellectual capacities, emotional fragilities, and symptomatic health issues. Yet while volumes have been written on the human condition, spawning even more volumes of self-help books, we rarely think of organizations that way. In fact, we tend to idealize how organizations *should* work, and we become impatient when transformation is not achieved quickly, formulaically, or permanently. Idealization is seductive; just ask anyone who is in love. When it comes to organizations, though, idealized notions of how they are "supposed to work" inevitably crash into reality, and paralysis is often the result. Once paralysis sets in, the work of alignment stops, as does any forward motion.

By way of illustration, the following embarrassing memory comes to mind. There was a time years ago when my son and daughter, both in grade school, were aspiring basketball players. A former player myself, I was pleased and proud to teach them some of the finer points of the game. In an enthusiastic moment, I attempted a move that the kids would surely recognize as worthy of a superstar like Michael Jordan. It involved dribbling to the basket and jumping as if laying the ball onto the backboard. Between the dribble and the ball touching the backboard, I would make an enormous jump and pass the ball under one leg before snapping it from one hand to the other. For players in their teens, this is standard playground stuff. Attempted by an increasingly sedentary middle manager in his forties, it could best be described as alarming.

My son rolled his eyes in disgust and said simply, "Ridiculous." He went on to point out that my right foot, which I was convinced had been dramatically elevated, had never actually left the ground. The muscles required for execution were not fully aligned with the intentions or memory of the mind. Furthermore, I hadn't practiced that move in decades! Clearly, my mind had made a promise that my aging body couldn't keep. Given all those circumstances, how could I have reasonably expected that my body and mind would gracefully align in service of the objective? The simple answer is that I had expected too much and had failed to do whatever I could to increase the odds of executing the move successfully. Organizations, too, have to be prepared and aligned for all the parts to work in concert toward a shared objective. If leaders haven't made the necessary preparations or have set expectations too high, trouble is bound to follow.

As my basketball story shows, even though a single human being has only one mind and one body, keeping them aligned is staggeringly difficult. This alignment is even tougher when you're dealing with a living, breathing organization made up of many bodies and minds. When the external environment is also dynamic, as in a rapidly changing and highly competitive marketplace, establishing and maintaining alignment is even more complex. Throughout the situations in this book, you will see a bias toward identifying those insights and behaviors that serve to maintain alignment within the company and especially between managers and employees.

The second fundamental belief informing this book is that each of us sits in a prison of our own perspectives, which is built on a base of personal experiences and behaviors. Our prison forms a lens that magnifies our particular set of beliefs and through which we come to see the world. Put another way, we are prisoners of our own minds, and we see new situations with the biases of past experiences. We must be aware of those biases as we wrestle with new situations. Only by being open to circumstances that do not fit our mental models can we make room for new learning and much more effective leadership.

That's where I'm coming from in this conversation about leadership. Now let me map out where I propose to take you in the pages that follow.

This book is organized into three sections. In Part I, "The Human Factor," we'll consider why people in organizations are so often brilliant as individuals—but collectively underwhelming. We'll see that individuals have both instinctive and learned impulses that tend to guide their actions. For example, harboring a personal agenda and looking out for self-interest are natural; so are seeking zones of safety and provoking or avoiding conflict. Most employees would also say they want to have an impact, contribute in a positive way, and be recognized and rewarded for their contributions. All these individual elements play with and against the momentum and direction of the group, and conflicts can be either disruptively blatant or dangerously well hidden. The situations discussed in this section are meant to help you recognize the push-pull of human nature in business and how you as a leader can channel the inevitable tensions in a positive direction.

Part II, "Situational Awareness and Judgment," will place you center stage in a variety of common business situations, from a product launch to a staffing dilemma to a crisis in a customer relationship. The judgments the managers in these stories make—or fail to make—have implications far beyond their immediate problems. Each manager's ability to define and manage process, discern the unique details of the situation, and understand the specific motivations of each team member are the keys to success or failure.

In Part III, "About Alignment," we'll put all the pieces together to see how leaders can use their understanding of individual motivation, group behavior, leadership awareness, and situational judgment to establish and maintain organizational alignment. The key is in managing expectations and cultivating perspective. If the principles laid out in this book can work in situations as complex as a corporate acquisition or the relationship between a CEO and the board of directors, it's probably reasonable to assume that they will work for you in your day-to-day business life.

One final thought before we dive in: anyone who tells you there's a simple recipe for superior leadership is either naïve or a liar. Leadership is hard and requires courage. Despite the popular tendency to trivialize the hard work of leadership by reducing it to a menu of bromidic recipes—"Just listen to your customers" or "Win the hearts and minds of your employees"—it is the exercise of courage that distinguishes great leaders from lackluster ones. This was the essence of the Pulitzer Prize-winning book *Profiles in Courage* written by President John F. Kennedy. In the following passage, he expresses his conviction that courage is situational and personal:

> To be courageous, these stories make clear, requires no exceptional qualifications, no magic formula, no special combination of time, place and circumstance. It is an opportunity that sooner or later is presented to us all. Politics merely furnishes one arena which imposes special tests of courage. In whatever arena of life, one may meet the challenge of courage, whatever may be the sacrifices he faces if he follows his conscience—the loss of his friends, his fortune, his contentment, even the esteem of his fellow men—each man must decide for himself the course he will follow. The stories of past courage can determine that ingredient—they can teach, they can offer hope, they can provide inspiration. But they cannot supply courage itself. For this each man must look into his own soul.

[*Profiles in Courage*, John F. Kennedy, Harper Collins, 2003, p. 256]

Part I
The Human Factor

I

Hardwired for Drama

There are few things wholly evil or wholly good. Almost everything ... is an inseparable compound of the two so that our best judgment is continuously demanded.
— Abraham Lincoln

Whatever opinions you may hold about the Civil War in the United States, most professional and even armchair historians agree that President Lincoln was an effective leader in the face of a conflict that threatened to destroy the very essence of the United States. If you study his behavior, you see that he attempted to avoid drama in the way he thought about people and issues. He tended to probe beneath the apparently obvious solution to a problem until he found one he considered sensible and practical. Relying on the conventional wisdom of the day or getting swept up in the polarizing political rhetoric of a divided nation was not his style.

That's not an easy line to walk, either in the 1860s or today. Drama appeals to something basic in us, whether it plays out on television, in the headlines, or in the boardroom. The tendency to oversimplify, too, is deeply ingrained in the human psyche; it probably serves some essential survival purpose, helping us to distinguish between friend and foe in a dangerous situation, for example, or helping us make faster decisions in a crisis. But in everyday life, oversimplifying can cause problems. Just ask a trial attorney how often potential jurors pick the apparent hero over the apparent villain, even before they learn the complex nuances of a case.

As Lincoln suggested, drama and oversimplification don't work in your favor as a leader. One reason is that they narrow thinking rather than expand it. A business discussion can start to look like a caricatured debate, polarizing participants into either an affirmative or a negative position relative to the conventional wisdom about the situation at a particular moment in time. Meanwhile, the most positive choice may lie hidden among all the momentary details, invisible to those who are looking only at the surface. Effective leadership requires skill in navigation, answers are often found in the situational details, and it's usually more helpful to make a series of thoughtful operational judgments than to seek a quick fix.

Here, for example, are three pieces of conventional wisdom. They all sound good on the surface, but if they're swallowed whole, without any situational understanding, they can lead bright and well-meaning managers down a rat hole that's hard to climb out of.

Conventional Wisdom #1: Employees are naturally motivated to do what the company needs them to do. All they need is an inspiring leader who listens to them and to the company's customers.

Having observed several companies try to restructure and grow, I have come to the conclusion that everyone has an agenda of self-interest. It varies from employee to employee, and it may show up as any number of things: a thirst for compensation, work assignment, recognition, learning, a more comfortable office, and so on. That said, employees are not the same as their self-interest, and various situations may influence their choices. For example, it is not unusual to see a longtime employee operate in defense mode to protect his or her position, while a new hire may assume more risk when doing the same job. The new hire may lack institutional knowledge and organizational savvy, but she also has little attachment to the status quo and so may be more open to disruptions that will ultimately help the company.

Leaders, too, are powered by self-interest. They enjoy the respect and stimulation they get from guiding a business to success, and they also want to protect their positions and compensation. In an ideal world, the leader's self-interest will be linked firmly with the advancement of the company. Effective leaders find ways to bridge all the self-interests involved in the equation—their own and the employees', as well as the best interests of the company.

Contrary to conventional wisdom, it takes more than an inspiring mission and a charismatic leader to motivate employees. Any leader who thinks the secret of good management is simply to listen to employees and customers is essentially picking two sets of heroes and ignoring the subtle interactions of multiple self-interests, including the leader's own.

Conventional Wisdom #2: A company's success is just a matter of its leadership.

We have all seen sports teams go from one coach to another with very little improvement in the lackluster results that spurred the leadership changes in the first place. The same thing happens in companies. Contrary to conventional wisdom, poor results are not solely the fault of the leader; a dynamic leader can be cut off at the knees if the organization doesn't know how to follow.

The reality is that many employees will never be in a formal leadership or even supervisory role at work, and nonmanagement employees typically outnumber management employees by a factor of eleven to one in the US workforce. [US Department of Labor, Bureau of Labor Statistics, Current Population Survey, 2010 data] What's more, most leaders are required to be followers in some situations, and followers need to be leaders in some settings. The point is that leadership and followership are equally important, both require development, and both skill sets develop best through situational experience. Yet the conventional wisdom encourages us to see only the leadership part of the picture and even to trivialize its practice while ignoring the followers who give the term *leader* its meaning. The company that habitually spends millions of dollars recruiting and cultivating its executive team while ignoring the training and development needs of its middle managers and nonmanagement employees is apt to get caught in a vicious cycle of executive changes and chronic organizational underperformance.

Conventional Wisdom #3: Employees come to work seeking simply to do their assigned jobs within the range of desired behaviors.

While employees may be motivated by self-interest, they also want to be part of a team. They want to contribute and be rewarded. In other words, people are hardwired for drama while inspired by a greater good. The dramatic tension between the two forces is almost palpable in organizations. Employees are pulled by the force of drama and negative swirl. At the same time, they are susceptible to—and may even yearn for—the positive emotional fervor created by a compelling mission and greater purpose. This story illustrates the point.

Decision Point: Introducing a Nonthreatening Way to Discuss Employees' Behavior
Some employees' behavioral styles are quirky, counterproductive, and even destructive. It is the leader's job to understand and address negative behaviors in a way that is unemotional and supportive, with the ultimate goal of effecting lasting behavior change in specific ways. In the following story, a new CEO used the Nexus of Behavior and Choices to create a common vocabulary and set behavioral expectations for her new leadership team.

Illustrative Story

During the first year of a public company turnaround, the new CEO brought in a new team of leaders. They came from a variety of backgrounds and had been successful in a variety of situations. They were all committed to the greater good of the turnaround and the development of a new company.

A turnaround is by nature an exercise in drama. The days are long, with full steps forward and half steps back, so momentum can be elusive. After the CEO had been in the job for three years and delivered the company's first profitable quarter in five years, she had to admit that the senior team had not fully congealed. They were individually strong and considered themselves good team players, yet they frequently came to the CEO with complaints or claimed to be victims of poor execution elsewhere in the organization. Seeking to break this behavior pattern, the CEO constructed a framework for discussion built upon a fundamental premise: in the absence of strong or corrective leadership, human beings gravitate to drama and blame. She drew the diagram below (Figure 1.1).

Figure 1.1: Nexus of Behavior and Choices

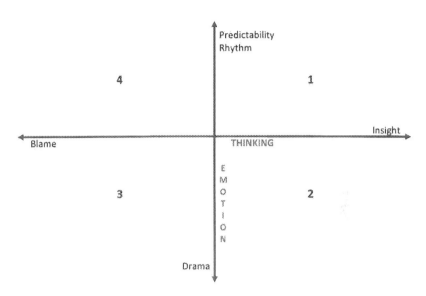

The horizontal axis (Thinking) denotes the spectrum of choices dominated by thought and judgment. On the positive (right) extreme, thought is driven by insight and learning. On the negative (left) extreme, thought is bounded by blame, loss of control, and so on.

The vertical axis (Emotion) denotes the spectrum of choices dominated by emotional response. On the positive (top) extreme, emotion is modulated in a predictable rhythm, measured and controlled. On the negative (bottom) extreme, drama reigns.

Now let's take a closer look at the four quadrants in this model.

Figure 1.2: Nexus of Behavior and Choices

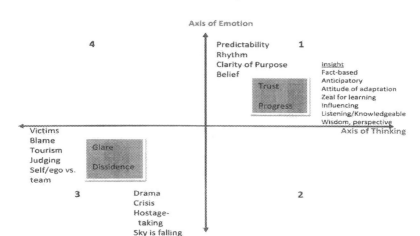

In Quadrant 1 (Trust and Predictability), on the axis of emotions, behaviors are characterized by predictability, clarity of purpose, and strong beliefs. On the axis of thinking, behaviors are characterized by insight, fact-based decision making, anticipation, adaptation, and wisdom. Behaviors in this quadrant are especially productive in public companies, which are rewarded for profitability. Choices made in this quadrant lead to trust and progress.

Quadrant 3 (Drama) represents organizations or individuals characterized by dissidence. Problems may go unsolved for long periods while organizations or leaders blame one another or see themselves as habitual victims of circumstance. Each day brings a new level of drama as the sky is falling or crises stack up. While teams in Quadrant 1 gain energy from progress, leaders and teams in Quadrant 3 lose energy with every successive crisis. To state the obvious, this is an undesirable outcome. Yet if you think about it, we live in a world where our natural proclivity for drama is fed and exercised daily. Media thrives by constructing simple winner/loser scenarios in the most complex situations, or by tantalizing the public with manufactured cliffhangers on "reality" TV. People in many parts of the world are virtually bombarded with drama, and as media consumption data shows, they love it.

We humans are so prone to drama that we make up our own stories in the absence of facts. A Wall Street financial analyst I spoke with recently described his mission in covering a stock this way: "Analysts don't need to be wrong or right; we just need to have a point of view. We prosecute, and the buyers judge." As he saw it, providing good advice was not his goal. The goal was to have and communicate a point of view that would precipitate action, that is, buying or selling. Investors would construct their own story to fill in the gaps. His objective was to produce a reaction, and the mechanism for doing so was coverage. This is not surprising, considering that brokers make money on transactions!

Quadrant 2 (Call to Arms) is interesting. Leaders who choose to behave in this quadrant, such as a leader who deliberately creates a "burning platform" to inspire change, may be making a good choice for the situation at hand. However, even an insightful discussion may be a poor choice if it generates unwanted fear. Behaviors in this quadrant may be compelling, but in the absence of control, they can lead employees into a swirl of speculation, drama, and even dissidence.

Quadrant 4 (Hopelessness) is also interesting. Consider an employee who thinks he or she is invariably a victim, constantly blames others for mistakes, and is convinced that everyone else is underperforming. These people are often burned out, and they drain others of energy. Left unsupported, their health may suffer, sometimes to a debilitating degree.

People in Quadrants 1 and 2 are generally reliable and can be expected to progress, if they choose their behaviors deliberately and control them intelligently. People in Quadrant 3 require leadership or redeployment. People in Quadrant 4 require help. People whose behavior is stuck on the left side of the chart despite reasonably persistent efforts to help them should not be working for you. They will sap the positive energy of their colleagues and coworkers, and they'll ultimately detract from the company's bottom line.

The CEO found the Nexus of Behavior and Choices to be a helpful management tool. She used it when she asked her direct reports to reflect on how they had behaved in various situations. If they were truly to lead the organization, she suggested, they should strive to operate consistently on the right side of the diagram. Over time, this tool became a commonly understood and nonthreatening mechanism for discussing behaviors and choices. It helped leaders avoid the dramatic trap of describing people and events as good or evil, right or wrong.

By the way, unlike many two-by-two matrices, this one doesn't take as gospel that Quadrant 1 is always best. I learned that from personal experience. Several years ago I came home from work, and my wife told me she had been diagnosed with two serious, chronic ailments. At that moment, she was understandably in Quadrant 3. My natural response was to use behaviors from Quadrant 1. I sat her down and calmly asked one question at a time:

"What exactly did the doctor say?"
"What do we know for sure?"
"What don't we know?"
"What are the next steps?"

In hindsight, this approach may have been calming for me, but what my wife needed was a hug. In other words, at that moment she needed me to be in Quadrant 2, embracing her drama. I certainly felt I was being courageous in facing the facts head-on, and I was eager to learn the details (at least the details that mattered to me), but if I had stopped to think about where my wife was emotionally, I would have used a very different process.

2

Tourists, Gatherers, and Collectors

We all know that everyone is different. We have our own hopes and dreams, strengths and weakness, personalities and emotions shaped over a lifetime. Even so, we behave more like some people than we do like others, and branches of social science including sociology, psychology, and anthropology couldn't survive unless there were some truth in the notion of "types" of people. In this chapter, we consider three types who are probably on your payroll: tourists, gatherers, and collectors. Let's start with the **tourists**.

I grew up in a small town on the New Jersey shore. Every summer, we watched the tourists invade. They hit the beach with pasty bodies, set up their lounge chairs and coolers, burned quickly, and left the beach riddled with empty cans and wasted sunscreen tubes. The tourists came to our town for a weekend of exuberance and went home Sunday evening physically spent and emotionally calmed. On Mondays they told stories of riding the big waves, outdrinking the locals, and performing athletic wonders in pickup basketball games. While they were back at their offices bragging about their exploits, our beach cleanup crews worked all week in preparation for another onslaught. We considered tourists one of Nature's less appealing creations. As we saw it, the tourists gobbled up the best of our town and left nothing of value. But to them, their weekends were just plain fun.

Now let's leave the beach and enter the workplace. Think about the last cross-functional team meeting you attended. How many people were there, and why were they there? How many said they would be glad to help but really didn't know very much about the situation and so couldn't add much to the discussion? How many were there only because they didn't want to be left out? How many were there simply so they could speculate later about who might get in trouble for something that was said or done? How many probably won't bother to go to any future meetings because they "didn't get anything out of" the last one? In other words, how many tourists were in that meeting?

There are two other types who might have been in your meeting. One is the **gatherer**. I have a dear friend who calls himself a gatherer of watches. He doesn't know much about them, but he finds them beautiful, and owning them makes him feel good. It's harmless enough. In a business setting, though, gatherers aren't always so benign. They come to the table with a specific and self-interested agenda, and they listen for and share only the information that is likely to advance that agenda. For example, maybe you know someone who fiercely believes his group should have a larger budget and therefore is hyperalert to "evidence" that groups with more money are spending unwisely. Now, a gatherer may actually have a legitimate purpose in mind. Maybe his or her boss asked the gatherer to attend the meeting and bring back specific information related to that group's work, for example. In that case, rather than crowd the meeting with noncontributing gatherers, the meeting organizer could simply include that person when the post-meeting notes are distributed.

The third type is the **collector**. The collector is like an expert whose passion is her collection of fine watches, who knows the genesis of each watch she owns, who made it, the name, number, and provenance of the movement, and so on. She not only buys watches; she repairs and restores them, writes about them for watch-lovers' magazines, teaches a class about them at the local community college, and sometimes sells them to other enthusiasts. Where others see simply an attractive timepiece, the collector's knowledge and insight add meaning and value to each watch and to the other people who share her passion. In other words, she doesn't just gather information; she also gives it, and in doing so adds to the collective understanding and insight of the community.

Decision Point: Identifying the People Who Will Add Value

As a manager in charge of a new project, whom will you invite to be on your team? Do you want people who have tackled this kind of project many times, or is it more important to have fresh ideas and a clean slate? Are there political considerations such as people you think you "shouldn't" leave out, even though you aren't sure what they'd bring to the conversation? Do you think the team roster should change over time, or are you looking for people who will stick with it to the end? This story suggests one way to think about who should be on the team.

Illustrative Story

At 4:00 a.m., a customer's network went down. It stayed down for ten hours, the longest outage this customer had ever experienced. The customer's CEO called Joe's CEO at noon. "We run the largest network in the world," the customer's CEO snapped, "and we stand or fall on our reputation for reliability. Do you have any idea how much revenue we lose for every hour the network is down?"

Emotions ran hot on both sides. Joe's company was the world's largest provider of network equipment, and their reputation, too, was at stake. Joe was asked to marshal the forces of the company to fix the problems and get the relationship back on track. He immediately called his counterpart at the customer's head office and launched efforts to solve the problem, but it was clear after several failed attempts that more than routine action was needed. Joe began to pick his SWAT team members. At 3:00 p.m., he convened the team's first meeting. The room, designed to hold twenty people, was overflowing with bodies. All of the CEO's direct reports showed up, each with one or two directors in tow. Even Joe didn't know everyone in the room.

Joe briefly stated the facts as he knew them, described the customer's point of view and state of mind, and summarized what he thought was still unknown about the incident. Then he went around the table, asking for additional insights. The head of sales spoke first, bemoaning what would happen to revenue this quarter if the problem were not fixed immediately. The head of quality said she was there to help, and while she had nothing to add, she wanted it on record that the company's quality metrics for the quarter would tank as a result of this incident. The head of R&D was sure this would turn out to be a customer operations problem, as most outages occurred (she said) when customers tampered with the topology of the network; she believed all of this could have been avoided if the customer had taken the last software upgrade. One of the directors of manufacturing and logistics showed up to see if there were spare-parts issues. After everyone else had been heard, Bob, an engineer in the back of the room, spoke up. He had no insight into this particular incident, he said, but he knew the customer's network in depth and had a list of questions he thought the team should be starting with.

It didn't take long for Joe to realize he had a mixed audience. Most people in the room knew less about the situation than he did and didn't have anything to contribute, not even questions that might jump-start the process of finding a solution. Some were there simply so they could tell others what had happened at the meeting. These were the tourists. Later that day, they were overheard in the cafeteria talking about who had attended the meeting and who hadn't, who might get in trouble because of the outage, what the impact on their quarterly bonus might be, and whether or not they'd bother going to any future meetings. Not one of them mentioned the customer.

Now take the gatherers. They came to the meeting to protect their self-interests. Their agenda was to advocate the suggestion that perhaps the outage was due to a customer error, not due to an equipment problem. They came to gather information that would protect their comfort level, preserve their perceived zones of safety, and shift blame away from their particular domain in the company. In some situations, gatherers can do great harm to a business. Can you imagine the impact if word reached the customer—or a competitor—that the company thought the outage was the customer's fault?

Finally, there was Bob, the knowledgeable collector who came to offer insight into what the team needed to find out next. He was seeking to collect valuable pieces of information so that in return he could bring specific value to the customer by getting their network up and running again. Bob's self-interest was fully aligned with the customer's interest.

Since the team would be meeting several times per week until the issue was resolved, Joe realized he needed a more focused kind of participation. First, he made sure there would be no tourists at the meetings. All who attended were required to participate, offer insights and remedies, and have the resources and empowerment to do what they said they would do. Next, Joe explained to the gatherers that the company could not afford to assume the issue was the customer's fault; instead, they had to find substantive answers by conducting an official failure-mode analysis and a subsequent postmortem on what went wrong: people, process, product, etc.

Over the next two weeks, the facts emerged: the product had not functioned appropriately when the customer performed a routine but infrequently used procedure. If Joe was going to keep the customer's trust throughout the failure analysis, he would have to make sure no one was in denial, so he made that his top priority in working with the team. The immediate problem was successfully diagnosed and resolved, but the inquiry pointed to deeper network issues. Joe put a tiger team in place, with a three-year deadline to build a more reliable network. New people, new processes, and new product designs would all be required. This wasn't going to be an overnight fix, so stamina would be essential. In the end, the tourists were quickly culled; most of the gatherers lost interest and were replaced by collectors who created value through customer intimacy and engineering insights. Interestingly, there had only been one real collector in the original meeting, but collectors accounted for nearly 75 percent of the tiger team. By paying close attention to the meeting dynamics, Joe was able to construct the best team for the job.

Smart leaders recognize the value collectors bring and make every effort to hire, retain, and reward them. But no company is comprised entirely of collectors. As a leader, you will have to deal with your ranks of tourists and gatherers, too. Joe successfully directed the gatherers away from their perceived zone of safety and down a designated path that led to customer satisfaction. He made sure they knew what they had to do and why, including why it was in their self-interest to follow his direction. After that, they were able to do what was needed, although they needed a lot of coaching and consumed a disproportionate amount of Joe's time. Joe realized he couldn't have very many gatherers on the three-year tiger team.

The point of this story is that we as leaders have to identify the basic nature of our trusted employees and make judgments accordingly. Surrounding ourselves with those who generally operate in Quadrant 1 of the Nexus of Behavior is the first step in increasing overall company efficiency and potential profitability. The next step is to encourage and support the collectors as much as possible.

Smaller companies or fledgling startups, for whom the priority is survival, tend to edit tourists from their midst pretty quickly. However, in larger companies, where managers have history and position to protect, an environment that favors the survival of tourists and gatherers frequently evolves. Tourism tends to become especially prolific in larger companies that are inattentive to culture and performance management. Active and conscientious leadership is the way to stop this. Organizations that build a system for cultivating collectors, redirecting gatherers, and purging tourists will achieve greater longevity and success.

3

Peewee Soccer in the Conference Room

Sometimes the best-laid plans in business go awry simply because the leader fails to manage group dynamics intelligently. Think about what can happen in a crowd: A crowd can quickly become a creature in itself, acting and responding in a seemingly unpredictable way, very much in the moment. The group exerts a strong force on the individual, who must decide quickly whether to join the group psyche, resist it, or become inert until the "right" choice becomes clearer. The same thing can happen in a company when the leader mismanages or fails to appreciate the power of the group psyche in a decision-making situation.

Before we look at the illustrative story for this chapter, let me give you a nonbusiness scenario that many people are familiar with: young children playing peewee soccer. Around the ages of seven to nine, children are just learning the game. They have an undeveloped understanding of field position and little awareness of the position they are supposed to play. So as the ball moves across the grass and begins to slow, perhaps approaching a sideline, all of a sudden parents may notice a rather large cluster of children hovering around the ball. Tiny legs flail in all directions, although no one is actually making contact with the ball. In one game I witnessed, the goalies left their stations to join the cluster. With the goal unattended, an inadvertent kick turned into a scored point. For the team that lost the point, the lure of the crowd mentality had proved disastrous. For the team that scored the point, although the outcome was favorable, it was a fluke, neither controllable nor repeatable.

Decision Point: Establishing Process
These days, passion and personal accountability are highly prized qualities in the workplace. Have you ever had to rein in an exuberant and well-meaning employee, even as you worried that you might be stifling her energy by doing so? When in doubt, it can help to focus less on the employee and more on the effect of her behavior, especially when that behavior has an impact on customers. We see that in the following story.

Illustrative Story

In his biweekly staff meeting, David, head of sales, took his team to task for what he felt was insufficient engagement with the customer. He had drawn that conclusion because most of the customer issues he encountered pointed back to products that did not meet the desired requirements, the promised specifications, or the production and delivery schedule. The staff meeting ended, and the bad news traveled fast.

After such an indictment from the head of sales, the R&D and manufacturing teams suddenly felt considerable pressure. Simon, the

CEO, supported David by chartering a new customer intimacy initiative; this didn't just add a new acronym—CII—to the company's long list of acronyms, it mandated new metrics, additional customer visits, and more. Although they were grateful for the support, the sales team did not trust the engineering teams to meet their commitments, so they didn't really want engineers talking to the customers. Moreover, rumor had it that the engineers refused to listen to customers, sometimes going so far as to accuse them of wanting the wrong thing. I've seen this kind of friction in large companies more times than I can count.

One month later, Simon flew to David's location for a face-to-face update on the CII. The R&D and manufacturing teams said they had missed their metrics, and they blamed sales for it. They said the sales team had refused to set up customer visits. The sales team said things were working just fine and that engineers' talking directly to customers was the last thing they wanted.

The functional groups, each in their respective silos, had dug in their heels. The sales team had become one crowd, with its own set of group actions and responses to the situation. The R&D and manufacturing teams had become an additional—and antagonistic—crowd.

Simon listened to the feedback, but he didn't mince words. He made it clear that these actions and responses were completely unacceptable. He told the teams that their attitudes had to change, and he took them to task for their seeming complacency despite the lack of progress. Simon basically lit a fire under everyone and told them to get cracking, a perfectly natural response. But was it the best one?

Let's look at what happened next. After the meeting, there was a frenzy of activity. Developers called customers to ask if they could visit. They called sales managers, and sales managers called developers, all looking to schedule meetings to discuss the situation. The manufacturing teams ran lengthy data reports on customer complaints. The head of quality control was told to develop a customer satisfaction survey. Within a week or two, customers began complaining that they were being bombarded by calls from one new person after another. They said they found the onslaught both disorganized and disruptive. Sales blamed R&D for setting unrealistic customer expectations and promoting products that were unavailable. Morale on all the teams began to falter.

Simon decided to see for himself. During a visit to one of the company's top customers, he was told:

"Simon, we want your company to succeed, but your teams are inconsistent. Some deliver on time, and some don't. In general, your lead times are too long, which makes my people feel that you aren't being responsive to our needs. When we have bugs in our products, it takes forever to find someone who knows enough about the products to help us. We don't have the right conversations with your company about new products you have on the road map. And lately, so many of your people are calling on us that we have no idea who does what anymore."

On the plane home, Simon was frustrated. The father of an eight-year-old, he realized that his team was subjecting an important customer to the peewee soccer syndrome. And while his intention was honorable—to improve customer intimacy—the teams working for him were mobilizing via an all-players assault on the ball, leading to customer confusion and organizational chaos. His own teams as well as the customer teams were suffering. In short, despite Simon's efforts, he had merely made things worse by lighting a fire under his teams without taking the extra step of more clearly directing their actions. Sure, it's natural to tell teams to get cracking, but how you do it can make the difference between an adverse reaction and a smooth, positive progression to solving a given problem.

Simon called David and Chris, David's vice president of sales, and they plotted a strategy. The sales teams would ensure that the top engineers, the manufacturing heads, and all members of senior staff had access to customers. Each account leader would build a customer relationship map that drove executive contact with assigned customer executives at least twice per year. Product managers who needed help validating product specifications would work through the sales teams to go on approved road shows with preapproved materials for which the sales teams felt expectations could be well managed. All product and delivery issues would be logged through a central tracking system to ensure they were captured, and both resolution and time to resolution would be documented. When this early-warning system indicated a problem, the critical account process, driven by David, would make sure the system and the company's leaders were aligned, to ensure that all resources would be directed toward effective intervention.

Over the next six months, things improved dramatically. The teams had learned that pursuing an initiative in the absence of a well-defined process to accomplish that initiative leads to undesired results. Through disciplined orchestration and practice, all players internalized the game plan and learned to play their respective positions. The peewee soccer syndrome ended, and David was finally happy with the level of customer engagement. Active leadership is an imperative in any successful company. However, it isn't enough to simply set activity in motion; that activity must be structured, understood by all, and monitored to its conclusion.

Without a doubt, Simon needed *courage* to listen to the customer's feedback without getting defensive. However, it's also clear that choices of *process* and *detail* drove an initial false start followed by a corrected and favorable outcome.

4

Too Many Demands or Too Little Discipline?

Sometimes the behavior of adults in organizations can be traced back to the habits and reactions they learned decades earlier. Here's an example.

Perhaps your daughter is going through a challenging period. Her homework doesn't get done; her room is a disaster area; she never has time for meals; and she forgets to take showers. She says she has too much to do. And what's the point of making her bed anyway? She's just going to mess it up again when she goes to sleep. One response might be to go along with her, hoping tolerance will ease her through this unfortunate stage more quickly. So you don't make a fuss about bad grades; you stop complaining about the state of her room; you figure that you're saving money on hot water because she won't take a shower; and you give her extra money so she can eat out. That response isn't likely to improve things. Whether it's with children, friends, or pets, tolerating the unacceptable generally leads to new areas of unacceptable behavior.

If you impose discipline, in most cases it's likely that your daughter will eventually reverse all those behaviors and even find time for piano lessons. From your daughter's point of view, she has been faced with a significant choice: she can embrace the value of the discipline and accept her obligation as a member of the household, or she can distance herself by judging the activities as not worthy of her time.

Once you know what to look for, it isn't hard to spot those employees who react to perceived excessive demands by distancing themselves and judging others or even the work itself. More difficult is helping them recognize their counterproductive behavior and accept that they have made an overt *choice* to disengage.

Decision Point: Managing Workload

At one time or another, most of us have been overwhelmed by a sense that we would never be able to catch up with—let alone get ahead of—the demands on our time. We can't even cross off all the items on our to-do list, let alone keep the list from growing longer by the minute. Often, though, it turns out that the sheer number of tasks isn't the real problem; the real problem is that we haven't done an intelligent job of prioritizing, and we haven't considered other ways to get some of the tasks done. Multiply that phenomenon by the number of people on a team, and you may find yourself where Amy is in the following story.

Illustrative Story

When Amy took over the helm at a new product management firm, she quickly saw that there was trouble. The engineers blamed the product managers and sales for never saying "no" to new product requests, and sales blamed the engineers for consistently missing launch dates. The product managers blamed everyone except themselves. In short, Amy had a behavioral mess on her hands that was harming the profitability of the company and quite possibly threatening its longevity.

Amy asked her department heads what they thought should be done differently to improve the way the company operated internally and externally. Without much reflection, most said they needed to hire more people or drop seemingly unprofitable products. Amy had a powerful and assertive personality, but she had learned to listen and then to think carefully about what she was told. She knew that gems of wisdom were often hidden in otherwise unhelpful chatter. So she asked her managers if making the changes they suggested would enhance the company's profitability. They responded that high-level concerns like profitability were above their pay grade.

Swallowing her anger, Amy went after the details:

- What is our documented product development road map for the year?
- How many dates for product launches were made on time in the past year?
- How many introductions of new products did we miss, and by how much?
- What kind of design-win progress had they observed?
- How many of the first installations or qualifications were made successfully?
- What percentage of development resources was being spent on new items versus fixing problems from the past or finishing just-released products?

Amy knew she had reached a crucial decision point. Her new teams were looking to her to fix things. She also knew that they were convinced they were being asked to do too much, though nobody said so. Should she lay down the law, read them the riot act, lighten their workloads, or simply fire the lot of them?

Had Amy been a less experienced CEO, she might have reacted negatively and felt completely justified in doing so. But she decided to give the matters at hand more thought, especially since she wasn't sure what steps she should take next. If she fired the managers, she'd shake up the company even more, and that would probably harm profitability in the short run. In the long run, she knew the company would settle down and profitability would be restored to previous levels, so she decided against taking drastic action that was possibly unnecessary at that point. The behavior and attitudes of the managers were totally unacceptable, but she understood that sometimes you have to live with the unacceptable until you find a sound way of making necessary changes. Amy reminded herself that she had identified a key problem area in the internal functioning of the company and was prepared to take action; and that gave her the courage to move ahead.

Amy's next step was to visit a representative set of customers. Here is what she found:

- The stated road map had not been shared with the customers.
- Customers felt that the company almost always missed product launch and ramp-up dates. They also expressed deep dissatisfaction with the general manager responsible for executing launches and ramp-ups.
- When dates were missed, the delays lasted for multiple quarters at a time.
- Design wins were sporadic, depending mostly on timing.
- More than 90 percent of the development resources were focused on fixing issues from the past or fixing problems in the most recently introduced products.

After Amy finished her customer research, she turned her attention to identifying patterns associated with the most onerous quality control problems. After talking with employees across the company as well as with important external partners including manufacturers, she found several common issues:

- Specifications were often incomplete and ambiguous.

- Vendors were sole sourced with unacceptably high-risk or nonexistent supply chain management processes.
- Team members were geographically dispersed, and communication was poor across teams.
- In almost no case was a single point of accountability identified. Programs drifted without a forcing function.
- The agreed-upon product development process was often disregarded.
- Program monitoring was insufficient.
- There was an absence of design for manufacturing and new product introduction work. Inventions were launched into manufacturing, and the yields brought huge startup distractions and killed the company's ability to deliver.

Amy's external and internal research led her to conclude that the highest-impact solution would be to focus on doing things right the first time. Even if she decided not to launch any new development programs, the R&D team would still be fully employed fixing products of poor quality. That was as unacceptable as everything else. Amy decided it was time to go back to basics, improve the quality of the gestation of new products, and free up more people to do even more new programs. Perhaps most important, Amy learned that no one on her staff acknowledged the unhealthy unit integrity and institutionalized denial. If her managers couldn't see it, did she also have a fundamental leadership gap to contend with? Yes, but not everyone needed to go— only those who were choosing to stay disengaged.

Slowly and patiently, Amy worked with her managers. Together they established systematic procedures and policies for all phases of product development and quality control. Rather than resort to mass firings or group scoldings, she eventually fired only the most recalcitrant members of her team. Whenever possible, she promoted collectors from within the company to fill the newly vacant positions. When she hired from outside the firm, she made sure they were collectors, too. She realized that she couldn't afford gatherers at this stage, and she avoided tourists at all costs.

Amy also resisted the impulse to lighten the load when her teams initially said they had too much to do. Instead, she worked with them to solve the systemic operational problems, and then she actually *increased* the workload by adding new programs for innovative product design.

As a leader, you will no doubt face similar situations. Your first inclination might be to change the entire management team or lighten their workload by hiring a cohort of consultants. But if you take time to examine the situation carefully, you may opt for a balancing act that keeps the best people in the fold. In business as in parenting, there is virtue in sound thinking, calm and unemotional responses, and deliberate efforts to improve both yourself and your organization through discipline and focus on both short- and long-term objectives. It isn't easy, but it works.

5

Hiring Winners

Making outstanding hiring decisions isn't easy. That's why large firms have professional human resources departments to help managers navigate the matchmaking process. A great candidate on paper might not be so great in person. In addition to the right skills and the right fit for the organizational culture, there has to be chemistry, an affinity between you and the person you will trust to maintain and build profitability for the company. Key hiring decisions for your team are your responsibility, even if your HR department does the heavy lifting or you delegate the task to someone else.

In making staffing decisions, two deceptively simple principles apply: First, it's not the quantity of players on your team that counts; it's the quality. Second, people get hired for what they know and fired for who they are, so consider both aspects of talent when you interview candidates. You want great, not just good enough.

Decision Point: Making the Best Possible Hire
Selecting and managing the talent on your team is one of the most difficult responsibilities you will face in your career, whether you're a first-line supervisor or a CEO. Reacting to the pressure to hire quickly, whether it's to get work done or to beat a budget cut, is one of the most common mistakes that managers make—and they and their teams pay for that mistake many times over. Building the team is very different from filling a job vacancy, as the following story demonstrates.

Illustrative Story

Jim had just been called into Tom's office. Tom was Jim's boss, and he was a surly curmudgeon. You know the stereotype: the guy with his feet up on his desk, an unlit cigar in his mouth, politically incorrect in just about every way.

"Hey, kid, I have a proposition for you," Tom said. "How would you like a free resource? I'm looking for a place to put Carl. You know he used to be a department head, and he's a bright guy, but I need some new blood in that job. You wouldn't even need to use one of your headcount allocations. What do you say?"

Jim was flattered and excited. The transfer was done the next day.

For a month or so, Jim felt pretty good. His group was expanding, and his boss had confidence in him. But he was beginning to notice that Carl wasn't getting along well with the rest of the staff. Carl liked the sound of his own voice, and when things weren't going well, he would pontificate at staff meetings about how screwed up the company was. He would cite chapter and verse about how things used to be done. Some members of Jim's staff started asking why Carl had been brought onto the team. Jim defended his decision because he was sure it validated Tom's confidence in him. Besides, who turns down a free headcount?

At the request of some of Carl's coworkers, Jim identified a few projects that would give Carl focus and keep him from disrupting the team. Month after month, he asked Carl to report on his projects, but there seemed to be very little progress. Jim began to lose the respect of his team; they saw him as a weak leader who was unwilling or unable to hold Carl accountable. Eventually, the team's negative impressions went from qualitative to quantitative; it was time for the annual upward feedback survey, which let employees express their opinions about their supervisors without fear of reprisal. When Jim received his team's feedback, he was shocked to see low scores in several areas, including hiring and driving results. This was an unpleasant first for Jim, who had always received glowing reviews from his team members. Before he hired Carl, Jim had been seen as an inspirational leader.

Jim's low feedback scores caught Tom's attention. They started having performance discussions, and Jim worried that he wasn't just losing the respect of his team, he was also losing the respect of his boss. He felt himself taking a defensive stance in many situations, and his family, initially concerned, began to be openly annoyed by his glum mood at home. Jim found himself remembering the days when people saw him as an up-and-coming young manager, one of the best and the brightest. He no longer felt that way, and he didn't think it was a coincidence that the negative changes began shortly after Carl joined the team.

Jim knew he didn't want to dump a low performer onto another manager to deal with, so he decided to begin the process of managing Carl out of the company. He began to resent Tom, feeling it had been morally weak of his boss to suggest that Jim take Carl on. But Jim knew he was the decision maker now, and it was time to set things right again. The next day, Jim called the head of human resources. Together they defined specific performance criteria, a set of conversations he would have with Carl, and a set of targets that Carl would have to meet or be terminated. Jim immediately felt better. He was confronting his problem, not living with it. He knew it would take time to resolve matters with Carl and restore his own good standing with his team, and that strengthened his determination. He would ensure that all future hires were highly qualified and committed to ongoing learning, teamwork, accountability, and adaptation. He would never again make the mistake he'd made with Carl, whom he eventually fired. Jim's mood at home and in the office improved markedly after that.

As Jim coached his team and managers for the future, he made it clear that each newly hired employee was expected to be great, never just good enough. Great might take longer to recruit, but Jim now knew that team morale, productivity, and his own reputation would suffer if a bad hire were made. If it is true that like hires like—or worse, that B players hire C players to avoid competition—then hiring errors will propagate over time. Jim set the expectation of zero-error tolerance when it came to building the team.

Hiring managers often settle for second best, especially if the priority is to get a job filled quickly. But the cost to the organization can turn out to be unaffordable. Taking the time to find the best possible hire may cost more for recruitment as well as for ongoing salary and benefits, but the higher quality and productivity will greatly offset those perceived extra costs. Factor in the morale-sapping influence a substandard performer can have on a team, and it clearly makes sense to hire only great talent for all positions.

6

Tribal Rituals

Forming tribes is human nature and probably goes back to the days when our forebears called caves home. The inclination of like people to gather in self-protective groups continues today. As a leader, you use tribalism to your advantage when you encourage employees to identify with the company, especially when rallying the team to fight a competitor. Identifying with functional organizations and work groups can be useful, too; people with similar jobs have a better shot at understanding one another, and mutual understanding often encourages collaborative behavior and team cohesion. Of course, all of that assumes that the team is properly managed. If it isn't, all bets are off.

Managed poorly, tribalism can do great harm to a company. Just as tribes can and do go to war, so too can teams within a company. Intracompany hostilities aren't usually overt, of course; they typically manifest themselves more like a coal fire burning deep underground for months and years, eventually undermining the mountain above. If each team that works for you views itself as an autonomous member of a loose confederation floating in a nebulous larger entity, there can't be any sense of the common good.

Internal surveys can give you an idea of where your teams stand. I know from personal experience that survey results can be eye opening, like a splash of cold water in the face when you're sound asleep. But you and your customers need your company to operate as a cohesive whole.

If the truth is that it's more like a bunch of tribes or factions, you need to know.

In a perfect world, promising anonymity to your survey respondents wouldn't be necessary, because employees' sense of personal accountability would be stronger than any fear. But businesses are far from perfect worlds, so promising anonymity—and making sure you keep that promise—will increase the odds of getting honest responses. I have taken this personally, by the way, ever since a former boss of mine invited candid input and promised anonymity, and then posted my comments, along with my name, on the company bulletin board. I remember the incident as if it happened this morning rather than some twenty-five years ago. That gives you a sense of the lasting damage a leader's betrayal of trust can cause.

Here are some survey questions you can ask your employees:

- Is teamwork strong in this company?
- What is the model or metaphor for teamwork in the company?
- Are you a strong team player?
- Are your peers and superiors strong team players?
- Why did you answer these questions the way you did?

Sadly, it is not uncommon to get responses like these:

- Teamwork isn't strong enough here.
- We don't really have a model for teamwork, and I don't know what you mean by "a metaphor."
- Well, *I'm* a strong team player, but …
- My superiors are jockeying for position, and my peers are out for themselves.
- When it comes right down to it, politics defines teamwork around here.

With this as a sobering backdrop, let's step into a business situation and see what it reveals about building a cohesive team instead of a confederacy of conflicting tribes.

Decision Point: Identifying Destructive Dynamics
Not all destructive behavior is easily visible. Sometimes, in fact, it looks quite benign. In companies and industries that have undergone significant change, especially prolonged contraction, many employees have learned to keep their heads down and their mouths shut. They figure they have outlasted multiple executive regimes and will outlast the current one, too. When organizations revert to self-protective tribal behavior, it is very difficult for the company to excel. Sometimes dramatic intervention is required, as we see in the following story.

Illustrative Story

Susan, the new head of human resources, was attending her first meeting of the CEO's direct reports. She was impressed by how friendly everyone seemed. After the meeting, she set up one-on-ones with each of them. She kept notes on her interviews and studied them in the evenings. As she reviewed her observations, some patterns began to emerge.

All the executives were very willing to discuss problems in their own area as well as in areas their colleagues were managing. The organization had just gone through several years of downsizing and cost reductions, and Susan detected a put-upon, victimized tone in the comments. While the mood at staff meetings and operations reviews was almost unfailingly amicable, in these one-on-ones, every executive identified at least two peers as problems that needed to be purged.

Next, Susan noticed that when issues were put on the table, they had a common ring: "Well, sales was unable to …" Or, "We designed it right, but ops couldn't manufacture it …" Or, "Customer support just didn't apply the right resources for the customer …" Or, "Development still isn't listening to us, and this is what happens …"

Susan noticed another similarity. The leaders who made these comments attributed the problems not to individual colleagues but to organizations within the firm: sales, operations, customer support, development, and so on. Susan knew that when true teamwork exists, people use one another's names and don't hide behind the impersonal labels of functional organizations.

Susan realized that teamwork in the company was very weak at best. At worst, the respective teams were like tribes in an uneasy truce or engaged in guerilla warfare behind the scenes. As she examined the data, it was obvious that a pervasive passive-aggressive dynamic was present throughout the ranks of upper management. Managers were overtly supportive of one another in front of the executives, but privately they were destructive and didn't hesitate to stab one another in the back. She noted this observation in red ink, resolving to come back to it when she had a more complete picture of what was happening inside the company.

Next, Susan began to look at organization structure. She learned that Rick, the head of sales, thought the developers were unfit to speak with customers. Based on that premise, he had taken on a liaison role, listening to the sales team and proposing product requirements for the development teams. He then forwarded those requirements to the marketing team for reference. But Susan discovered that Rick wasn't the only liaison in the mix. John, the development leader, thought the sales and marketing organizations were impotent and ineffectual, just as Rick thought John's developers were unfit to speak with customers. Acting on this belief, John chartered a group of product managers and technical product managers to interface with the marketing team. The marketing team then interfaced with Rick, who in turn spoke to the sales team. Then the sales team would speak with the customers.

Susan drew a flowchart depicting the dynamic, and when she was finished, she stared at it in horror. Although every executive clearly believed that customer responsiveness and development coherence were poor, they all took great comfort in having isolated their organizations, convinced they were isolating themselves from the impotence of the others. It didn't surprise Susan in the least that the company was losing money.

Wondering what other coal fires were burning under the surface, Susan studied the backgrounds of her peers so she could understand the assumptions and agendas they brought to their jobs. She saw that the present company had become what it was after absorbing more than twenty other companies through mergers and acquisitions. All the growth had occurred in the past ten years, and sixteen of the acquisitions had happened in the previous five years. As a result, every functional organization supported some projects that were still run by the same people who had worked on them before the acquisition. Often those people still worked in the same buildings and with the same colleagues. Organizations had been combined and centralized, but that wasn't enough to drive a new culture.

Even though the acquisitions had taken place many quarters in the past, employees had never been offered the opportunity to make an overt choice to join the acquiring company, nor had they been individually recruited. Only a small number of executives on both sides had made an explicit choice to join the acquiring company, and they had encouraged or "rerecruited" one another. Below the executive level, employees saw themselves as a part of a loose confederation of tribes. While they complained about the company culture (or lack thereof), in reality they had no sense of or desire for a common culture.

Susan realized she could help the CEO understand the passive-aggressive behavior of the team leaders and the cultural journey they would have to make together. To start, the CEO would need to make a thoughtful assessment of the competence of the executive team. Were these executives really team players? Did they have the ability to lead? Further down in the organization, managers would effectively have to recruit all employees, no matter where they came from, to sign on with the company as it existed in the present. The effort would unmask the stubborn hangers-on, too. Employees who remained wedded to the tribal nuances of the past would have to go.

Then Susan made a list of the most important common themes that emerged from the data she had gathered:

- Pervasive blame or victim syndrome (lack of accountability)
- Passive-aggressive behavior (say one thing and do another)
- Organizational complexity in structure or practice
- Hiding behind impersonal function designations instead of using people's names
- A pathology of myths inflating an employee's self-importance. For example, Susan heard the following more than once: "Since I'm still here, I must be a top performer. All those downsizings got rid of all the low performers on my team. My boss had the guts to make the tough decisions. But on other teams, it's a different story!"
- Unwillingness to deal with unsatisfactory performance or counterproductive behavior
- Confederation of tribes rather than explicitly recruited team members

Susan knew she had to act decisively. Over the next two years, more than 80 percent of the senior staff was removed. Their replacements brought the skills needed for future growth rather than the skills that had served the markets of the past. More important, the new managers were explicitly recruited into the company of the present and the future. Susan led a series of training sessions to articulate the new culture and the behaviors that would define it. The sessions were experiential and interactive, inspired by Susan's conviction that people can't think their way into a new corporate culture; they must *act* their way in. That would mean changing behavior and practicing the new behavior over time, acting as a team, reinforcing and correcting one another's behavior. Managers cascaded the principles and assessments through all levels of the organization, using a template-based communications plan designed by the corporate communications team. Organizational complexity was reduced by rooting out such legacy chokepoints as multiple interfaces to other interfaces. Engineers and product managers were required to speak directly to customers, facilitated by the sales team.

Within thirty-six months, the company became pro forma profitable, market share increased, and the stock price grew tenfold. It was a long, painful, and necessary journey, and the first step had been Susan's. By taking the time to study the words and behaviors of the organization's leaders, she was able to identify common themes, extract the root causes of failing productivity and profitability, and finally enlist the CEO in a plan to break the patterns and move forward.

Not every example of tribalism is going to be so easy to spot, but as a leader, it's up to you to keep an eye open for the first hints of such behavior among your teams. If you see it, take immediate action to eliminate the problems that are causing the behavior. You can't afford to tolerate negative forms of tribalism, the age-old tendency of groups to fight other groups. Make your improvement actions visible; make sure that everyone sees you examining operational practices, questioning organizational structure and soliciting feedback from employees. Then communicate the new culture, celebrate role models, and show that the entire leadership team is on board. If you do those things, problems like the ones Susan faced won't get out of hand in your business.

7

Letting Go

We've all heard the saying, "If you want something done right, do it yourself." What that really means is that you think others lack your level of skill, and you wouldn't trust another person even if you thought she did have what it took to do the job right. This kind of distorted self-esteem often goes with the territory for highly talented, driven, and intelligent leaders, especially in cultures that revere individual achievement and heroic stories about underdogs succeeding despite near-overwhelming odds. But you'll have to resist the I-can-do-it-better syndrome if you're going to cope with the pressures and time constraints you'll face as your company grows and prospers. Besides, since most of us today work in an environment that sees general management and functional specialization as separate but equally valuable career paths, you will inevitably reach the point where you literally can't do your employees' work yourself. Even if you had the time, face it: you don't have the skills.

Delegating is one of the most difficult things for strong leaders to do. Many highly successful leaders continuously fight the urge to micromanage. The best ones understand that micromanaging is counterproductive, and if the only way they can delegate is to force themselves, that's what they do.

Imagine you're a technically proficient leader in a rapidly growing company. Every day, your job seems to become more demanding and complex. Eventually you have to make a choice: Do you delegate or not?

If you delegate, how can you ensure the superior quality you insist upon and still rise to the challenges of your role? You may feel as if you're at war with yourself, your instincts pitted against your common sense. Developing leaders must navigate multiple tensions, including:

- Confidence versus paranoia (Do I trust my people to do things well?)
- Depth versus breadth (How do I want to be known as a leader? Which jobs do I want to be considered for?)
- Technical versus managerial (Am I willing to leave the lab and become a generalist?)
- Individualistic orientation versus team orientation (Do I privately believe others drag me down?)

Decision Point: Learning to Delegate
At the heart of most problems with delegating, you will find one of three root causes: the need for control; a genuine belief on the part of the leader that he or she can do everything better than anyone else; or a leader who doesn't trust anyone on the team to take the handoff. (That lack of trust may be either justified or unjustified.) Learning to delegate requires building a team in which you can have confidence, and understanding that as you advance in an organization, sooner or later you will find yourself in a role where you don't have complete subject-matter expertise. The next story features a smart engineer who got in over his head because he lacked leadership skills and refused to delegate.

Illustrative Story

Phil was a gifted scholar, with degrees from the top engineering schools in the country. His academic background and leadership in standards bodies made him a recognized expert. People admired his confidence. He was an individual contributor who had always derived great satisfaction from going deeply into a technology or an idea. Now that he was in his thirties, though, he was becoming interested in broader managerial assignments. When he envisioned his career path, he figured his strong technical knowledge would position him well for a next assignment as vice president of engineering for a startup company. A position like that, he thought, would give him the control he enjoyed as an individual and also the experience of directing a team of engineers.

Phil got the job he wanted, but he quickly ran into trouble. His confidence and narrow expertise put him in conflict with the head of sales, who thought Phil and his team didn't listen to customers.

"Phil's team thinks they know best," the head of sales complained at a staff meeting. "They're developing what they think customers should have, not what the customers are asking for."

Phil believed he was following the right path and there was no need to change. This not only annoyed the head of sales, it raised a red flag with Phil's boss. To make matters worse, Phil was running into problems with his own team. He hated giving performance reviews, and he was unwilling to remove poor performers. The best members of his team began to resent Phil's lack of leadership and grumbled that the poor performers were dragging them down. Instead of asking for help or dealing directly with customers, Phil retreated into an emotional bunker. Then he started seeding his own political agenda, suggesting that sales was not prioritizing what his team needed or selling what they had. As tensions grew, Phil's team members either took sides (tribalism) or withdrew completely to their zones of safety. Their productivity plummeted.

Then came Phil's performance review. In addition to assessing Phil's performance against his objectives for the year, Phil's boss rated him on a scale from 0 to 5 in each of several leadership attributes. Phil's form looked like this:

Phil Gordon – Annual Performance Assessment

Get results: 3
Recruit and nurture the highest-quality team (hire and develop): 2
Build the company of the future: 2
Demonstrate teamwork: 1
Possess and develop deep industry knowledge and insight: 4
Plan effectively and lead successful execution: 2
Evidence good chemistry, trust, and alignment: 1
Demonstrate open communication: 1
Drive focus: 2
Establish credibility with all, internally and externally: 3

Phil was stunned. Most shocking to him were the low scores on teamwork, trust and other people skills. He scored especially low in areas related to relationships and leading change. He realized he had lost his connection with his followers and had no feedback system that would have let him know how he was really doing. He wondered whether it might even be too late to redeem himself in his boss's eyes.

His boss acknowledged that Phil knew his stuff and was a smart guy, which was why he'd hired Phil in the first place. But the fact that Phil wasn't a good leader had become painfully obvious to most of Phil's peers and superiors. Phil's boss said it appeared that Phil didn't know how to delegate, motivate, or work across organizations with department heads and customers. To Phil's relief, his boss suggested a leadership coach. Grateful to be given another chance, Phil agreed to see the coach right away.

The coach, whose name was Mary, began by asking Phil whether he truly wanted to explore his leadership strengths and weaknesses, or whether he was just doing it to please his boss and keep his job. Did he really want to understand his behavior? Was he truly committed to improving? Humbled, Phil made a commitment.

First, Mary asked Phil who his most important constituents were. He responded, "Sales, corporate functions—especially finance and manufacturing—and my development team."

Mary knew that with engineers a picture is worth several thousand words, so she took out a blank sheet of paper and drew this chart:

	Strategy	Architecture	Execution

Every leader, she explained, has to define three fundamental elements:

- a business **strategy** to sell a product or service;
- an **architecture** of the work to produce a product or deliver a service; and
- **execution** of the strategy to sell the product or service.

Mary knew that Phil had played football in high school, so she used this analogy: "Think about a professional football team," she said. "Their strategy might be to hold on to the ball as long as possible and not give the other team a chance to control the play. The architecture of work supporting that strategy might be to be known for the best running game for offense and the best defense in the conference. So the team would prioritize investments in favor of things that would help them run out the clock, like paying top dollar to sign the best defensive backs in the game. As for execution, the metrics would show clearly whether they were delivering on the strategy."

Then Mary populated the left side of the chart with the three constituencies Phil had said were the most important to his business:

	Strategy	Architecture	Execution
Sales			
Finance and Manufacturing			
Phil's Team			

Mary then asked him which of the three elements was most important to each constituency. Phil looked at Mary's chart, thought carefully, and then replied, "Sales wants to be inspired by the market opportunity and know that we have great products."

"Good," Mary said. "So they care most about strategy. What about the next group?"

"Finance and manufacturing want to know we will use money and resources wisely," Phil said.

"Okay, that sounds like execution to me."

"And my development team wants to know we have the best architecture and will win in the market."

Mary pointed to the blank boxes inside the chart and asked Phil to assess on a five-point scale how satisfied each constituency was in the area that mattered most to it. Phil felt that sales would give a low score on strategy, probably not higher than 2. Manufacturing and finance would rate execution a 3, he thought, and the development team might say they were around a 4 when it came to having a winning architecture.

	Strategy	Architecture	Execution
Sales	2		
Finance and Manufacturing			3
Phil's team		4	

Then Mary asked who on his team was the most credible and best equipped to make the case to each constituency. Phil replied that in all three cases, he would personally be the most credible. She told him she would do some interviews to reveal how his subordinates, peers, and superiors saw him. Whether or not he agreed with the responses, she said, perception was often reality. The feedback results would help him see the otherwise invisible barriers to his effectiveness as a leader.

The feedback validated Phil's impressions (although the sales score was actually 1, not 2). Mary told Phil that the best leaders of teams typically receive total scores of 10 to 12 out of the possible 15 (that is, a maximum of 5 for each of the three elements: strategy, architecture, execution). She went on to say that as the organization grew and became more complex, it would be increasingly difficult for Phil personally to be the main point of contact for each constituency. Mary was telling Phil that if he wanted to lead effectively, he would have to hire, and then he would have to delegate. That way, Phil would be able to scale as the organization grew in size and complexity.

As you might imagine, this was a crucible for Phil. His confidence crashed, followed by a growing realization that he had been dangerously blind to most of what was going on in the organization. To his credit, he was eager to learn what he had been missing and to take action accordingly. As he went through the process, the real Phil emerged, the person who had succeeded as an individual contributor and now sincerely wanted to become an excellent general manager. He learned to hire for talents that he did not possess, and he delegated responsibilities (although he still had to fight the urge to hover over his subordinates).

The prospect of dividing up his job to better serve his key constituents was hard to swallow, but it made sense. He hired a lead product line manager who would build a strong product plan and market synopsis to woo the sales teams. Her measure of success would be a sales score of 4, up from the current dismal 1. With the new manager in place and the objectives clear, Phil had more time to focus on product development and planning. To his surprise, he felt productive and effective for the first time, and he began to trust his team. He also quickly realized that he had an ownership problem to solve. He felt accountable for the overall strategy, but when he asked people whom they thought was accountable for architecture or execution, many different answers came back. Clarifying ownership would be his next challenge, and we'll look at a number of approaches to that challenge in Part II of this book.

Phil was back on the road to success, not because of his technical knowledge, but because he had become a better leader. He had learned an important lesson: many strong individual performers naturally resist delegating work, but as the team and the business grow, this can be a dangerous liability. If you're one of those leaders, or if you have some on your team, an effective way to break the pattern is to do a simple analysis of what matters most to each of your key constituencies and how well you think they would say you're doing, and then validate by asking them directly. The resulting picture will show you where you need to focus your efforts and where you need to bring in others who can do the job better than you could.

Not being able to do it all yourself is a good problem to have. It means the company is growing and that more varied talent and expertise are needed throughout the organization. Learning to delegate and then systematically support the people you've chosen to help you is an essential aspect of becoming a more mature leader. Your efforts will translate to a more successful business, and in the long run, like Phil, you'll feel not only more relaxed, but prouder of the contributions you're able to make.

As for the tool, when the sum of the feedback on these leadership threads is 8 or lower, results will typically begin to falter, and ultimately both the leader and the leader's direct-report team will be recast.

In this situation, it's clear that it took *courage* to give and receive unvarnished feedback. It also took courage to construct a *process* to deal with that feedback. The process of disaggregating the leadership role and assessing performance in turn provided a clinical and blame-free way to look at the situations and see *detail* that might otherwise have been hidden. In this story, the confluence of courage, process, and detail became a valuable lens through which Phil could finally see a path forward.

The Human Factor:
Looking through the Lens

In the preceding chapters, you've watched leaders navigate a variety of organizational challenges. Now I invite you to take a step back and look at their stories through the lens of courage, process, and details. These brief questions are intended to be provocative, not prescriptive. As you rotate the lens in one direction and then another, new images may come into focus.

Q. Why do you think the Nexus of Behavior and Choices in chapter 1 worked so well as a management tool? Was it because it gave the CEO the courage to talk about counterproductive behaviors with her team? Was it because it gave the team a common process for discussing complex issues? Was it because it gave the CEO a way to describe desired and undesired behaviors in greater detail than she had before?

Q. What's so bad about gatherers? Surely attending a meeting so you can take notes and bring information back to your boss isn't a bad thing, especially if the boss asked you to. As a manager, have you ever sent someone to a meeting simply so he could report back to you on what happened? What effect do you think that had on the other people in the meeting? Could you have sent someone else who would have contributed to the outcome in addition to taking notes?

Q. The key to success for Simon in chapter 3 was establishing a process to improve customer intimacy. But his team was split into factions that were busy pointing fingers at each other: manufacturing against sales, sales against R&D, and everyone swarming the customer at the same time. Can you think of a time when you had a critical problem to solve and a team you knew was dysfunctional? Did you have the courage to address the dysfunction, or did you go immediately to process and details and hope everyone would just shape up? How did it work out?

Q. In chapter 4, do you think Amy would have showed more courage if she'd chosen to lay down the law with some of her teams and lighten the workload for the others? Do you think the truly courageous decision would have been to fire the most divisive managers to show she meant business?

Q. In chapter 5, Jim initially addressed Carl's performance problems using a process-based solution. Why do you think it didn't work? Was the process wrong?

Q. Have you ever hired someone you felt was good enough and found that he failed within two years? At the time, did you consider that a hiring failure on your part, a performance failure on the employee's part, or something else? What do you think about it today?

Q. Chapter 6 is about the power of tribalism to strengthen or undermine a corporate culture. Susan saw tribalism as a negative force in her company, and she courageously conducted a thorough analysis (details) before designing an action plan that included a wide variety of interventions (process). Can you think of a situation in which tribalism is a positive force? How could you as a leader exploit it without pitting one group of employees against the others?

Q. Mary's process-driven approach in chapter 7 certainly appealed to Phil's well-developed left brain. Do you think that's why Phil was eventually able to change his leadership style so successfully?

Part II
Situational Awareness and Judgment

8

Managing Risk

In the military, soldiers are taught to maintain situational awareness at all times. The idea is to be constantly aware of what's happening around you and to anticipate what might happen next so you can be ready. How accurately you can anticipate depends on both what you're seeing in real time and what you've learned in similar situations over time. The right combination of current situational awareness and past experience will help you make the right situational judgments at any given moment.

The same ideas apply in the office. Indeed, some people use military metaphors when they talk about business, and this isn't entirely out of place. In business, there are losers and winners, campaigns and setbacks, strong positions and weak positions, leaders and troops. Through it all, you're constantly working to enhance your situational awareness so you can make better decisions in rapidly changing circumstances.

Most of the decisions you make as a leader will involve risk. Make the wrong call, and money may be lost, production schedules may fall behind, or a product ramp may be delayed. If a new marketing campaign confuses customers, the new products may languish in inventory. The list of potential risks seems endless, and insecure leaders can easily freeze in their tracks or be tormented by anxiety about whether the right decision was made. Confidence comes in knowing that risks can usually be managed, and if mistakes are made, there are techniques for correcting them decisively.

Part II of this book deals with issues related to situational awareness and judgment, and this chapter addresses the issue of risk. Let's meet Brendan, a product manager with two important products undergoing major transitions. In one case, he managed the risks and made the right situational judgments. In the other, well, let's find out what happened.

Decision Point: Managing a Successful Transition

In my own company, I recently shared the story you're about to read with our eighteen thousand employees. I wanted to know whether it sounded familiar and how they had managed similar situations in their own jobs. The responses were numerous, thoughtful, and passionate, and I was amused but not surprised to see that employees in different departments all over the world were absolutely sure Brendan's story was really about the project they were working on! (In fact, it was inspired by things that happened well before I joined my current company.) One employee wrote, "It is axiomatic that you don't dismiss a capability until you have an equal or better replacement." Axiomatic it may be, but the responses suggested that it's also rare. Effective transitions require discipline, and counterintuitive thinking may be needed.

Illustrative Story

Brendan's company was ready to transition from an old generation of product to a new generation. Since the new products could cannibalize sales of the older release, a debate arose on how to model the financials. Some people wanted to ramp the new product as soon as possible and simultaneously announce the end of life of the old product. But Brendan and some of his colleagues weren't sure that an accelerated market introduction would be best. As they saw it:

- The sales channels might be unwilling to retrain all their people quickly. If that happened, the new product might not be absorbed as speedily as hoped. Worse, the sales channels might stop buying the old product to keep from getting stuck with inventory. Instead of boosting sales, the strategy of ramping the new product and rapidly sunsetting the old one could tank sales.

- Customers might not want to certify the new product in their applications immediately, so the sales channels might compensate by introducing the new product more slowly. In fact, some customers might stock up on the old product to avoid running out. As a result, the new product wouldn't be absorbed for a long time to come.

Brendan needed to make a decision. He had consulted with his colleagues in an attempt to raise his situational awareness, but now he felt caught between two polar positions, no closer to a solution than before he asked the question. As he examined the details of the situation, Brendan saw that the old product still generated a significant and reliable revenue stream. He concluded that the best choice would be a slow transition rather than a flash cut. The slow transition would introduce the new product into an application not currently served by the older generation of product. Over time, the new product would be allowed to bleed into existing applications, but only as quickly as could be controlled and monitored.

The decision proved to be a very good one. Continued sales of the old generation product helped offset costs of developing and marketing the new one. Both the old and the new product found markets because the new product served an application that the old one didn't. Brendan successfully mitigated his risks and presided over a smooth product transition. If only that were the end of the story …

Things didn't work out quite so well for Brendan when the manufacturing operation for another product line was being transferred from Mexico to China. The Mexico factory was slated to close in six months. During the transition period, old inventory was sent to Mexico, and new assembly was sent to the facility in China. Demand for the product began to grow, something the team hadn't counted on. Soon orders were pouring in, but the team was driving a tight timeline to shut down the plant in Mexico.

Brendan had another important choice to make: Should he hedge his bets by delaying the shutdown in Mexico? If he did, the company would have no trouble meeting demand. The problem was that there were no contingencies built into the transition plan to allow for an extension of the closure period. Brendan felt boxed in. He knew the ideal solution would be to work out an extension, but he was being held to his metrics; so he shut down the Mexico factory on schedule. What's more, he did it before the new factory had qualified new parts or started making the product.

Based on the obvious facts alone, it would seem that Brendan acted irrationally. How could he possibly shut down a factory that was producing products that were selling well, without first making sure a new manufacturing facility was up and running? The answer is that leaders sometimes feel forced into making decisions they know are probably flawed. Sometimes this is unavoidable; in those cases, situational awareness and communication of the potential consequences will at least prepare the company to deal with the negative outcome. In Brendan's case, it would have been far better to fight for an extension, even if he ended up being overruled. Instead, he banked on the hope that the new factory would be fully operational soon enough to meet demand for the product. As you can see, his decision exposed the company to much more risk than if he'd been able to delay closing the old factory. He had fallen prey to the demand for speed in the transition.

In transferring the work from the old factory to the new one, some crucially important pieces fell through the cracks. The software processes used to monitor production in the old factory were not transferred; the product had essentially been "thrown over the wall" to China. The manufacturing recipe had been lost, and no research had been done to find out whether customers would be willing to qualify products manufactured in a new site. The product line was in disarray, and customer dissatisfaction continued to build for more than twelve months following the transfer.

Like a driver on the racing circuit, Brendan learned the hard way that the art of a transition is balancing speed with the leader's ability to control risks. Speed should be determined by how fast you can go while still controlling the path and outcomes, and thoughtful contingency planning gives you more control.

As a leader, you will face similar situations. You will feel pressured to adhere to what your gut tells you is an unrealistic timetable, and when things go wrong, you'll want to kick yourself. I've been in this boat many times myself. Sometimes it's unavoidable, but avoidable or not, it's never pleasant. The trick is to use a soldier's situational awareness to assess current conditions and look ahead to see if you can locate any potential landmines. The next time Brendan was asked to lead the transfer of a manufacturing facility, he used his past experience to inform his judgments. He planned well ahead, consulted his colleagues, and mitigated risk by building contingency mechanisms into the process at every stage.

One reality of managing risk is that it takes *courage* to see a situation in all its dimensions. Then you mitigate risk by putting in *processes* that let you look at the *details* and respond appropriately. Failure in courage, process, or detail usually results in unnecessarily painful outcomes.

9

The Planning Imperative

We plan all the time in our personal lives, figuring out what to buy at the grocery store, checking what to watch on TV at night, allocating the investments in our retirement portfolios. In business, sound planning is part of good leadership. Planning for product introductions, real estate moves, capital investments, and so much more occupies much of your time, and as the company grows, planning consumes an ever-larger part of your day and the days of your direct reports.

If your company has a set of plans and processes in place to address daily operations, potential problems, and future expansion, it's likely that the inevitable surprises will cause less stress and upheaval. Peewee soccer responses will be less likely. In other words, executing according to plan is a sort of insurance policy against managing by reacting. Shrewd planning is a specific skill, and not everyone on the team has it.

Decision Point: Creating the Right Plan and Executing It Successfully

---

Too often, senior leaders or others who are viewed as "big thinkers" design the strategy for a company or a project; experts in operations engineer the plan; and individual employees are then asked to fill in the blanks with metrics they'll work toward in their individual roles. At that point, the overarching strategy is largely forgotten, and employees simply get on with their jobs. The best strategic plans are created by people who not only understand the market and the company at a deep level but also have an active and enduring stake in the adoption and execution of the plan. Corinne eventually figured that out, as you will see in the following story.

Illustrative Story

Barkham Audio had just completed its eighth successful year, but the executive team was concerned that they didn't have an adequate plan for continued growth. Corinne had been successful generating sustained profitability in her previous company, so she was invited to develop a strategy that would sustain Barkham's growth well into the future. A number of vice presidents and directors stepped forward to help Corinne sort the issue out, and they seemed eager to work closely with her on the prestigious strategic planning project.

Corinne called an open meeting, inviting anyone who wanted to participate. But only about half of those who accepted the meeting invitation showed up. The volunteer from R&D was off dealing with a customer crisis. The manufacturing leader declined at the last minute, citing problems with yields on the factory floor. Other key players didn't bother declining; they just didn't come. Not wanting to lose time, Corinne held the meeting anyway. The group drafted a work plan, and action items were handed out to the attendees. When the next meeting came around, even fewer people were there, and none had completed any of the action items.

Corinne realized that she had set up a structure in which everyone reserved the right to participate but no one felt any responsibility for following through. Her resentment started to build. She was no stranger to conflicting demands; after all, she'd taken on this strategic planning task in addition to managing an existing product line. She knew the objective was important, and she wondered why those who volunteered to help out weren't helping at all.

Realizing that failure wasn't an option, Corinne dissolved the team and made a radical change in her approach. She looked for a small group of bright people who had a proclivity and passion for defining the future. They came from different parts of the company, but they were all compelling individuals who cared enough to be willingly conscripted. They in turn made a list of the brightest people in the company and used them to test ideas, collect competitive information and customer data, tease out knowledge gaps, and identify experts who could fill in missing information.

For the next thirty days, Corinne and her team met every evening from eight to ten to review new information and determine what additional data they needed. They continued to build concepts and test them with their stakeholders in a Socratic manner, asking questions rather than making pronouncements.

At the end of the thirty days, the team stood proudly before the CEO and his staff for an executive review. They had assembled a cogent view of the current and potential scenarios for continued growth in a highly competitive landscape, with more data and validation than any single person in the company could have developed. Arguments pro and con had been vetted well before the executive review, and there was a high degree of buy-in thanks to the incremental, customer-validated process the team had used to develop their recommendations.

The value of this team lasted well after the strategic plan was approved. The team members were now uniquely qualified to lead the company's next generation of product and program initiatives since they had the deepest insights and the richest network of internal and external relationships, and they could best explain the "why" of the strategy to the outside world. They had enhanced their reputations within the company and positioned themselves to make significant contributions as the company continued to flourish. They were also ideal "strategic ambassadors" who could inspire employee engagement.

If you volunteer (or are volunteered) to serve on a project team, find a way to stick with it in some way, even if it gets handed off to another team for execution. It's unlikely that the execution team will have the same zeal for the project that you do, and your continued involvement will inspire the ongoing emotional commitment of the employees called upon to do the work. Also, when something goes wrong, you'll have the institutional memory and situational awareness to identify and address the root cause of the problem. Finally, if you're leading a planning team and you attract a bunch of tourists and counterproductive gatherers, show them the door!

10

Schedule or Quality?

In Sun Tzu's classic, *The Art of War*, the author states that only the ignorant seek to live in a world of black or white. As we saw in chapter 1, Abraham Lincoln felt much the same way. Life and business play out in a world of indistinct and ever-changing shades of gray.

Do you remember Brendan? He knew he should have tried to extend the date for the factory closure in Mexico, given the high demand for his product and the uncertainty about whether the new factory in China could be up and running in time to meet demand. But he stuck to the original schedule because he believed that was the most important metric for the company, and he didn't want to fail. It was a classic example of black-and-white thinking, and as we saw, things didn't work out well.

One of the most difficult decisions a leader will be called upon to make is whether to drive for speed and schedule (even if quality may suffer) or drive for the highest quality (even at the risk of delayed execution and missed schedules). Product managers who are in charge of new releases face this dilemma frequently, but so do publication editors, advertising creative directors, building contractors, and sales leaders scrambling to put together presentations for unexpected customer meetings. Typically, the stakes in these situations are high, and leaders who see the answer as a black-and-white, binary choice—that is, schedule *or* quality—are stacking the deck against themselves. As we will see in this chapter, only by learning to maintain the right level of tension between schedule and quality can leaders deliver both.

It's a bit like a person who is struggling to lose weight and resolves to eat just one meal a day but then hears a dietician say that the one-meal approach is wrong, and people lose more weight faster by eating three to five small, balanced meals each day. At first the dietician's advice seems at cross-purposes with the goal. Yet in light of relevant details—what will be eaten, portion size, individual metabolic profile, and so on—the two seemingly opposing thoughts may turn out to be complementary. Details make a difference!

That said, time and again managers are forced to make decisions and set directives that prioritize schedules over quality. They're afraid that being second to market or missing a crucial customer demand will result in less long-term business. Yet when schedule trumps everything else, organizations find that responding to and fixing bugs over and over again is no fun, bad for morale, and not appreciated by customers. The question for managers is how best to navigate the tradeoffs. Let's see what that looks like.

Decision Point: Balancing Schedule Demands with Quality Requirements

Perhaps you have found yourself or your team dealing with what appear to be competing demands. It could be as simple as submitting a report with preliminary conclusions—before all the facts and evidence were gathered—or releasing a new product quickly, without completing as much testing as you and the team might have wanted. We make these decisions every day, and in the end, we realize that whatever decisions are made, for whatever reasons, our customers and the marketplace will judge whether they were right.

Illustrative Story

Bill, a development manager, was asked to drive a special program for his company. For the previous eighteen months, the company had pushed to gain share on a close competitor. Management wanted a new product that would really knock the competitor off balance. They considered acquisition targets, but none offered a killer product. So they asked Bill to come up with a proposal that would put a new product in the market within twelve to fifteen months. Schedule was crucial. Bill was up for the task and commandeered a team to develop the product on an aggressive schedule. He convinced the general manager to allocate special incentive compensation for his team, contingent on their meeting the deadline. He was sure this would add spice to the challenge.

Fourteen months later, the team shipped the new product to its first customer. The first month went well, with no negative feedback. The team was ecstatic. But soon the customer complained that the product was rebooting itself several times a day. With more than one hundred units in the customer's network, Bill had good reason to sweat.

Before long, the customer was irate, and memories of the sales team's hyperbolic product descriptions just fanned the flames. The service they had been promised and the revenues they had counted on were going up in smoke. After four weeks of failed attempts to stabilize the product, Bill admitted to his CEO that he was finding it hard to get to the root cause of the problems. Either each returned product showed "no trouble found," or he was told that it was probably a customer error. He was sent a software patch each week with the promise that this one would do the trick. Time after time, it didn't.

Since the development team seemed unable to provide insight, Bill engaged the general manager of the product business group. After another fruitless two weeks, the general manager decided to play project manager himself. He made the team stay late every night, and he asked them to list the features and capabilities in which they actually did have confidence. Much to his chagrin, he found the following.

- Specifications for each module were not completed, so there were ambiguities in inter-module communication.
- There was no joint hardware and software design review, which could lead to breakdowns at the interfaces.
- The hardware designs had been baselined using functional prototypes, but the elements typically used to ensure product robustness—timing diagrams, timing verification, signal integrity checking, and so on—had all been bypassed.
- No team members had been specifically allocated to isolate problems. As a result, problems were referred to hardware specialists who would say the issue was in the software. The issues were sent to the software team, who invariably pointed back at the hardware team.

Bill and the general manager decided to put the product on hold. The sales force wasn't allowed to take any new orders. Next, the general manager began to baseline the design again to understand all of its strengths and vulnerabilities. Even before he was done, he found that two-thirds of the circuit cards in the product needed to be redesigned. As Bill and the general manager drove their project plan, new leaders were brought in to focus on quality of design. Every trouble that had been identified by the customer was replicated and isolated, and only verified fixes were sent to the customer. Over the next three months the customer's expectations were managed week by week. The customer network finally operated to expectations, and the redesigned products consistently delivered highly reliable service.

The team continued to develop new products, but never again were they allowed to place schedule over quality. Eventually they realized that the real issue wasn't "schedule versus quality" at all; it was managing customer expectations. Together they drafted four operating principles, which they all taped up on the walls of their cubicles:

1. Do things right the first time. Process matters!
2. Quality isn't just how you develop and test, it's how you manage customer expectations. If you can't manage expectations, you'll have insufficient quality.
3. If you can't be honest with the customer about bugs, don't give them early releases (and don't expect them to trust you).
4. "Schedule versus quality" means nothing.

Before Bill left the special project, he asked a cross-functional team to quantify the costs of poor product quality, especially the cost of the unplanned time spent on remediation. Here's what he discovered:

- Customer visits and product-specific conference calls consumed twelve weeks of sales time.
- The technical support team spent twelve weeks trying to isolate problems.
- Software development also consumed twelve weeks.
- Hardware development and redesign ate up two hundred sixty weeks.
- Test resources consumed three hundred weeks.
- Other development took thirty six weeks.

- Executive engagement required twelve weeks.

Bill made the following assumptions:

- Sales, customer support, software development, and test professionals bill at $180,000 per year.
- Hardware engineers have a loaded labor rate of $130,000 per year.
- Executive management has a loaded labor rate of $360,000 per year.

Bill estimated that in total, the team had spent over $2.5 million unplanned dollars and lost in excess of an additional $80 million in sales of the product, and an amount of sales of other drag-along products. With gross margins of 50 percent, the net loss was the equivalent of over $42 million in sales, all due to poor quality. Bill didn't factor in the negative impact on other programs of having their people temporarily redeployed to put out Bill's fires, but a rough estimate, based on two other programs that had almost certainly been affected, was that it had cost an additional $40 million in sales. All in, the total cost of the problem approached $85 million. Bill was both gratified and horrified to learn that this was the first time any of the engineers and engineering managers had ever worked through an exercise like that.

Figuring out the estimated costs of dealing with the quality problem helped Bill's team see that speed (how much to be shipped by when) versus quality is a false dichotomy. There's no way to know the optimal speed of the schedule unless you have quality data. The key is ensuring that the integrity of the product and product yields are under control and trending favorably, and simultaneously managing the customer's expectations through frequent, fact-based, detailed communication.

Any schedule-versus-quality debate is a lose-lose discussion. Leaders must always drive to the highest quality and highest confidence designs. The best way to process and manage speed is by managing customer expectations. That takes communication, insight, and managing the details; it can't be delivered by an edict.

11

Reducing Glare

Imagine driving down a road with the sun directly in your eyes. The road under your tires guides you, to a point, but the simple fact is that the *glare* prevents you from seeing very well. The farther and faster you drive under those conditions, the more likely it is that you'll get into an accident. The solution is to eliminate the glare, put on good sunglasses, and slow or stop the car if necessary.

That's great advice for drivers, but how does it apply to organizational leaders? Let's be honest ... even when we're driving, glare from the sun is rarely enough to make us stop the car. Usually we just lower the sun visor and put on sunglasses. That's even truer on the job. The temptation is to keep going, thinking you'll figure it out on the fly, when a quick stop to take your bearings might be the better option. Staying with the car analogy just a little longer, changing direction can work just as well as stopping when you're trying to get out of a glare situation.

Decision Point: Recognizing and Correcting Blind Spots; Finding the Right Point of View
Sometimes employees are so comfortable in a familiar operational routine that they can't adapt to a new issue, so they keep doing what they've always done without seeing that the old routine is actually hurting the bottom line. This is especially likely when an established team takes on a new project, or when a leader with a successful track record moves to a new function or department. People tend to operate on the basis of the past without analyzing whether or not the details of the current situation are the same as the details of past situations. As in so many other situations, one of the hardest things in business is knowing what we don't know.

Illustrative Story

Consider a company (let's call it ApX) that made elaborate computing devices to process the content and flow of information. ApX had been selling its devices to one customer at a time and had become reasonably proficient at creating high-quality products. Out-of-box reliability generally hit 98 percent (three percentage points higher than the original internal target). Both the manufacturing team and the development team had become comfortable with those levels, and, in general, most customers were too, judging from customer satisfaction data from the legacy customer base.

During the past year, though, a new set of customers began to purchase a derivative form of those specialized computing devices. Twelve of the ApX products were used to deliver an end-to-end application. The failure of any one of them would lead to a service outage for the end customer. As the company released the new products, the out-of-box reliability was found to be roughly 90 to 95 percent, not unusual for new product ramps.

As the new customers began to adopt the devices and build end-to-end applications, they too were learning. Increasingly, customers felt a need for significant turnkey support. But, as the sales representatives explained, ApX was a product company, not a service company. The sales reps dropped the products off at the customer's facilities, but the reps weren't in the business of educating the users about the product. As the customer struggled, more and more problems arose. Some were errors; others were configuration subtleties that weren't documented for that specific application; and many were out-of-box reliability issues. The complaints came fast and furious. Finally, word of these issues made its way to the ApX CEO, Pat, who put the accounts into a problem-oriented triage mode.

Pat stepped up, bringing together leaders from across the company to deal with the issues. Much to her frustration, she was met with universal defensiveness and denial. The sales team blamed the product managers for not documenting application-specific configuration guidelines. The product managers said it wasn't their job to be experts in the applications, since they only developed the general-purpose devices. The product managers blamed manufacturing for delivering products with a high fallout rate. Just about everyone was convinced that the customer's engineers were not technically astute or disciplined in their operational practices.

The reality was that no one at ApX was in charge of making the customer's application a success. Instead, the teams were focused (and compensated) on making, selling, and shipping the products. Pat began to deconstruct the problem into actionable steps, making sure that customer expectations would be managed along the way. She asked the customer support team to document a joint ApX–customer operational practice. (This took some doing, as the customer saw no need to change its own practices.) Next, she asked the leaders of the product and consulting engineering groups to support a project whose goal would be to document and code configuration guidelines.

The next step would be harder. The manufacturing team was adamant that the out-of-box quality was generally excellent, even though the out-of-box reliability during the ramp was 90 to 95 percent. According to the manufacturing team, the explanation was simple: there just weren't enough logistics and support capabilities. No matter what Pat did or which lines of inquiry she pursued, one thing was clear: ApX was focused on making and shipping product as cost-efficiently as possible. That's what the company tracked; that's what the teams measured; and that's what everyone understood.

Then she did the math. In an end-to-end cascade of devices, the probability of a failure was calculated this way: out-of-box reliability factored into the number of devices in a given product cluster. So, with out-of-box reliability at 98 percent per device, a cluster of twelve devices would render an end-to-end reliability of 78 percent (0.98^{12} = .784 and change). But with an out-of-box reliability of 90 percent per device, the reliability of the cluster was roughly 28 percent (0.90^{12} = .282 and change). So, 72 percent of the time the customer would have an unsuccessful service launch with ApX equipment (100 percent − 28 percent = 72 percent). What the customer really needed was a cluster reliability of 95 percent, which would in turn require per-device reliability to be on the order of 99.6 percent. The problem was that ApX collected per-device reliability statistics, not cluster-level statistics. What's more, it tracked out-of-the-box reliability (rather than delivered service levels), which was meaningful to ApX but not to customers. It would take a lot of forensic work to understand just how to drive the cluster reliability where it needed to go.

In this situation, misalignment within ApX was pervasive and accepted, a classic state of glare. On one hand, everyone knew the customer was unhappy but did nothing about it, even though all organizations within the company had a strong incentive to improve customer satisfaction. Several factors were continuing to stand in the way of progress. Here's what Pat discovered:

- Accountability was unclear. There was no one throat to choke, so to speak, to ensure the success of the new application the customer needed.
- Organizational agendas were promoting defensiveness, denial, and finger-pointing.
- The problems did not naturally fall within the normal responsibilities of any one organization.
- There were no ApX metrics for service quality.
- The customer's expectations for success were inconsistent with the internal success model defined by ApX.

With the underlying root causes identified, Pat and the team drew up a systematic remediation plan that everyone could follow. As often happens, the remedy for glare conditions was ultimately found through a relentless examination of the details, driven by an inquisitive and nonpartisan leader.

As Pat's experience shows, when a company suffers from glare and doesn't realize it, making changes to solve the problem can be like pulling teeth. It can be just as painful, too. The first step is realizing that glare has become a blinding factor; the succeeding steps involve analyzing the practices that contribute to that glare and then making changes. Resistance may be fierce at first, but if you as the leader insist that the team make fact-based decisions with the customer's interests— not your organizations' interests—as their guide, visibility will improve dramatically. Glare will flash in your company—you may count on that. Your job is to watch for it and eliminate it before the problem entrenches itself too deeply in the way you do business.

This said, it takes *courage* to adopt the customer's view of an end-to-end experience instead of relying on more accessible (and often more easily rationalized) internal functional metrics. It takes a *process* to bring organizations together, aligning around an outside-in view of the system and agreeing to be measured as a total system. Finally, as Pat learned, in complex business situations, many problems don't naturally fit into the normal responsibilities of any one organization. Tending to the *details*, step by step, is essential to remediation.

12

Managing Customer Expectations

Attitude goes a long way in business. Show your customers sincere can-do enthusiasm, and chances are, they'll respond positively—or at least they'll give you the time of day. Radiate negativity and reticence, and that's what you'll get in return. Ultimately, though, attitude is only part of the equation. Hearty enthusiasm in an attempt to cover up problems is, obviously, counterproductive. When things go wrong, how well you manage your customer's expectations can make the difference between a temporary speed bump in the relationship and a customer who's lost forever.

I'm reminded of an acquaintance I'll call Keith. The last time I saw Keith was at his twenty-fifth wedding anniversary party. Twenty-five years of successful marriage is something to celebrate, even if Keith's guests were giving the couple the same quizzical looks they had given them at their wedding. You see, Keith and his wife weren't exactly equally matched when it came to charisma. By most conventional standards, Keith wouldn't have attracted many appreciative glances. What's more, some people found him boring. When I asked about his secret to a long and seemingly very happy marriage, he thought for a moment and said, "Well, right from the start I set my wife's expectations very low. She told me this morning that I had definitely achieved those expectations. Beyond that, we learned together."

I had to smile. I knew Keith was joking … at least, I think he was. But his point was well taken. He managed his wife's expectations from the start, and the relationship lasted. Properly managing expectations can help make the relationships with your customers last a long time, too.

Decision Point: Balancing Best Effort with Expectation Management

Nobody wants to disappoint a customer, and even the most honest leaders sometimes find themselves agreeing to a deadline they aren't sure they can meet—believing that they and their teams will rise to the challenge—or enthusiastically describing the full feature set that should eventually be available on a new product, even though it may be several releases and many months away. While that kind of behavior can generate a successful meeting or two, it usually leads to uncomfortable downstream conversations at best, and seriously damaged customer relationships at worst. The next two stories describe the tension between best-effort attitudes (can-do enthusiasm) and well-managed expectations.

Illustrative Story

Stuart was the leader of his electronics company's critical accounts program, and he had his hands full. Schedule slippages were pushing two very important customers to the breaking point, and they were complaining loudly. Stuart's consumer TV division had been working hard to develop a new set of technologies that would provide dramatic improvements in video quality for a broad set of products. The team had embraced a bold stretch goal and prototyped several machines that had earned awards and rave product reviews. Several customers were poised to buy the entire new product line, pending a successful manufacturing ramp.

Stuart's team members were thrilled by the response, but they knew there weren't any sure bets. They understood that they were inventing, which was why they had been able to develop prototypes with dramatically better contrast than any existing technology. From the team's perspective, they were involved in a breakthrough initiative. They would just keep putting one foot in front of the other, giving it their best effort to deliver the most innovative and highest-quality products as soon as possible. If production yields were poor, they would simply schedule more parts so they could meet customer demand.

Then several customers told Stuart they were planning production quantities for what showed signs of being a hit-or-miss Christmas season. There was a finite window of demand; if the team missed the window, both the customers' financials and Stuart's team's reputation would suffer a blow. Further, it appeared that yields were 15 percent, well below the 50 percent minimum required for profitability and the ability to meet customer demand. The team had already identified at least four substantive problems that needed to be remedied before production expectations could be met. As Stuart investigated further, he discovered that specifications were still in flux with the end customers as well as with his company's supply chain. That contributed to greater levels of unpredictability, production run after production run. Worse yet, some parts were sole sourced from smaller vendors that couldn't accommodate sharp spikes in demand.

The calls with customers became strained. On one hand, the development team was working at full steam, with a best-effort attitude. On the other hand, they had missed customer expectations numerous times. And although the team firmly believed their best-effort approach was customer centered, they had never completed a detailed risk analysis with risk mitigation and contingency planning. As a result, if any one thing went wrong, they would almost assuredly disappoint a customer, despite their good intentions.

To stabilize the situation, Stuart recommended a detailed triage plan that prioritized the technical problems they needed to address. He recommended improved cross-functional project management so that schedules took interdependencies into account. He also built in risk assessment and risk mitigation. To execute the plan, though, Stuart would need people with skills he didn't currently have on his team, so he replaced some of the leaders. He decided that if there were areas where the customer's skills were stronger than those of his own team, his team would rely on the customer to do the development. He worked aggressively with his peers in manufacturing and sales to secure better cross-functional engagement. Finally, he made sure that all specifications were codified and put under change control with customers.

Why was all of that necessary? After such a promising start, what had gone wrong? Put simply, the team failed to navigate the tension between best effort and managing expectations. Originally, they wanted to make sure they could be nimble in a rapidly moving market, so they decided not to be overly conservative in their approach. They chose the best-effort model, complemented by lots of interaction with the customers. However, some crucial elements just weren't part of their model: assessing downside risks, for example, and accounting for the realities of invention and scale. As a result, their risk mitigation and contingency planning were inadequate. In short, they saw their choice as binary: either rapid innovation (seen as exciting and good) or prudent risk management (viewed as conservative and bad). Had they thoughtfully assessed the situation, they might have been less likely to think in extremes and more likely to see that if they gave their customers an envelope (range) of expectations, they would be giving themselves more flexibility. Instead, customers repeatedly learned about problems and risks one at a time, and Stuart's team felt the pain as they struggled to manage their own expectations and those of their customers.

Best-effort approaches usually skip the important steps of considering risks, developing contingencies, and managing expectations. While it was obvious to everyone in this story that best effort wasn't working, it took more than intellectual acuity to make the change. It took courage. Let's build on that point with a more general business example.

Illustrative Story

Liz was the new CEO of a public company. The previous quarter had finished at the low end of the guidance range set by her predecessor, and the internal operating plan called for the company to grow 10 percent quarter over quarter. Eager to please the new CEO, the head of sales told her that he was on track to make the plan, but when Liz looked at his bookings she saw that they were down in the last quarter. It was clear to her that the company had, at best, six weeks of visibility, not twelve, for that quarter.

As Liz and her staff discussed how to set guidelines for the next quarter, here's what she heard:

From the CFO: "Liz, the Street is expecting somewhere between 8 and 12 percent quarter-over-quarter growth."

From the SVP of sales: "We're going to do our best to make double-digit quarter-over-quarter growth happen."

From the EVP of manufacturing: "Based on current order coverage and past conversions from new orders to in-quarter shipments, I just don't see any way of achieving double-digit growth."

From the head of the products group: "The roll-up comes in at an expectation of 1 percent quarter-over-quarter growth."

Liz knew that if she told the Street that the company would grow at only 1 percent quarter over quarter, the stock would get hammered, an inauspicious beginning to her tenure as CEO. She then asked if there were any quality or customer problems, or other items that could present significant in-quarter downsides to the numbers that each leader suggested. The head of sales identified three quality issues which, if not resolved, could have a large negative impact. The product leader named four potential issues, and the manufacturing leader identified several product lines where the yields were low enough to cause a miss.

When Liz added up the downside risks, she calculated that the quarter could actually come in 4 percent *lower* than the previous quarter. Given those considerations, Liz and the CFO needed to think about how best to manage investors' expectations. Much to Liz's discomfort, the only thing she knew for sure was what the investors wanted to hear from her in her first quarter as CEO.

As Liz saw it, this wasn't just a business dilemma; it was a question of character. She decided not to tell people what they wanted to hear, but instead to begin building a reputation for delivering facts and predictability. She established guidelines in the range of negative 4 percent to positive 8 percent, knowing she had the rationale and bottoms-up forecasting to justify both scenarios. Given the degree of uncertainty about the numbers and the realization that things could go wrong, communicating an envelope or range of possibilities seemed to be the best way to manage expectations. Of course, she knew that wouldn't be enough. Her job was to mitigate the downside risks and capitalize on the upside.

As we saw in both examples in this chapter, best-effort approaches are typically oblivious to risk management and mitigation. If leaders are to earn the trust of their stakeholders, they are better served by approaches that help them manage expectations using envelopes of downside and upside, always informed by risk-adjusted expectations. Beyond that, it takes courage to act as Liz did when she faced her first earnings call, or to make the changes Stuart made after figuring out what was causing the trouble with his critical accounts. The important point here is that managing internal and external expectations is crucial. Do it right, and life gets easier. Avoid it, and you'll have a very bad time indeed. The good news is that managing expectations is relatively straightforward: you just have to have good information, and you have to be willing to share it with your stakeholders.

13

Leader as Casting Director

As companies globalize and grow through acquisitions, they become a mosaic of corporate cultures and attitudes. In such a diverse environment, selecting the right talent for the job—never easy—becomes a challenge that requires a sophisticated approach. Should workforces be deliberately built through overt and specific casting of talent, or should staffing decisions be driven primarily by loyalty to existing employees? In companies that embrace the loyalty dynamic, you see considerable effort devoted to retraining and repurposing, and generally a low level of specialization. In casting companies, the energy typically goes into assessment, recruitment, hiring, and managing turnover. There are downsides to both models. In loyalty companies, employees may have a pervasive sense of entitlement and tend to resist change. In casting companies, there can be a twitchy atmosphere and more job-focused insecurity than business conditions warrant.

First, let's define terms. I use "casting" as it is used in the entertainment industry: important roles are deconstructed into the traits and attributes that are crucial for success in that role. In the movie business, those traits include box office pull, proclivity for playing victims or villains, aptitude for dramatic or comedic roles, and so on. The role is analyzed to develop a casting profile, and screen tests ensure that the selected actor or actress really is the best fit. Studio politics aside, loyalty means very little when casting a part; what matters is whether the actor or actress has the right stuff to play his or her role. I often see the casting model in Silicon Valley companies. When a startup is formed, the venture capitalists do their best to cast an A team that will maximize the probability of success for the new firm.

Of course, few companies have the benefit of starting from a metaphorical clean sheet of paper. Larger companies that evolve from virtual monopolies, for example, often have a bias for reusing people, thinking of employees as generic soldiers to be dispatched wherever the need arises. In these firms, employees can develop a sense of entitlement, up to and including a belief that the company owes them employment for life even when they intellectually understand that is far from true. Interestingly, I've seen this tendency persist in a company's culture long after its monopoly position has ended.

Decision Point: Loyalty or Casting?
Rewarding loyalty and longevity—a strong cultural value for decades in many companies and many countries—can be at odds with the tenets of organizations that think of themselves as performance based. Today, as the nature of markets and jobs changes dramatically, every manager, from the CEO to the first-line supervisor, will sooner or later ask, "Am I going to staff my team by casting, or do I believe in maximizing the job security of the workforce we have?" The answer isn't always obvious. What you as a leader decide will depend on the type of company you are running, your priorities for the company, and the kind of corporate culture you want to encourage. Let's take a look at Greg as he grapples with whether to take the loyalty or casting approach to some important staffing decisions.

Illustrative Story

A large corporation recently hired Greg as the product manager responsible for a product family that generated roughly $50 million in annual revenue. The economy hadn't been kind to Greg's company. Headcount on his team and in the company as a whole had shrunk by an order of magnitude over the past three years, creating considerable anxiety in the ranks. As he considered his employees as well as the teams he depended on for cross-functional support (manufacturing, sales, finance), he came to some stark realizations.

The product managers were highly skilled technologists with doctorates from excellent universities. They shepherded many products, some of which were on the road to replacing current products, but they had little or no skill or experience in business management. The famous case study of the Osborne Computer Corporation would have been instructive to them, if they had ever heard of it. Allow me to digress briefly and tell the cautionary tale of Adam Osborne.

Born in 1939, Adam Osborne was a visionary entrepreneur who introduced the first portable computer. It weighed twenty-three and a half pounds and sold for about half the cost of comparable nonportable machines. At its apex, the company was shipping more than ten thousand computers each month. Revenue soared from $6 million in 1981 to some $68 million the following year. Osborne filed a Form S-1, laying the groundwork for an initial public offering to follow six months later. IBM quickly introduced a faster product. In response, Osborne announced a next-generation product that would be faster still and available around the time of the planned IPO. The rapid competitive volley brought demand to a screeching halt. Buyers decided to wait for Osborne's new product, even though it was six months away. Sales of the first-generation product plummeted, and Osborne Computer was left sitting on massive inventory. The IPO never happened. To this day, technologists of a certain vintage use "Osborne" as a verb meaning to shoot oneself in the foot. If you're a technologist, the last thing you want someone to say is that you've "Osborned your current product line."

That brings us back to Greg. As he studied the team and its objectives, Greg came to understand there was a very real danger of Osborning his product line. The development team members were indeed highly skilled, but none of the leaders was adept in product development, project management, or design for manufacturability. For example, the finance leader was a former manufacturing production control manager with no formal accounting or finance experience, and the manufacturing leader was a former IT manager who didn't know the first thing about design for manufacturability.

All of the people supporting Greg's products had three key things in common:

1. They had survived a major and protracted downsizing.
2. They believed that the very fact of their survival proved they were contributors in the top 10 percent of the workforce.
3. They were loath to admit to themselves that they were in jobs for which they had no expertise, no awareness of best practices or disciplines, and no past or present mentors to turn to when questions inevitably came up.

Greg's revenue target for the coming year assumed 25 percent year-over-year growth. Given his findings, he had an important choice to make: Should he continue to perpetuate the loyalty model, seeking to develop the team he had, or should he start over? Starting over would mean redesigning the organization from the ground up, conducting a sort of casting call to find hunters for new markets and farmers to tend the profitability of the past.

The conventional wisdom as well as the operative culture in his company suggested that Greg should place a high value on the loyalty of his employees and send his team for whatever training they needed. But Greg realized the training process could take years, and there would be no way to deliver 25 percent revenue growth with a team of functional rookies, especially since he was not personally accomplished in all areas. While it took courage to buck the corporate culture, he put the best interests of the company ahead of the individuals on his team and decided to cast a new staff that would be better suited to meet corporate objectives.

Hoping he might be able to tap people elsewhere in the company rather than bring in all new hires, he asked his human resources partner to conduct a company-wide skills inventory. The results showed that sourcing from within wasn't going to solve the problem. The company as a whole lacked the essential skill sets of project management, product management, new product introduction, and design for manufacturability.

As disappointing as the findings were to Greg, they made sense in light of the company's history. The company had been a near monopoly, coming of age as the only major player in a growing industry. Nobody worried about competition; they just did the best they could to ship, and that was generally good enough because customers had nowhere else to go. Greg and the company at large would need to bring in excellent talent with new skills—one hire at a time. It would take months, but it had to be done.

You may be thinking, "Wait a minute … Greg didn't even make an effort to retrain his team! Was he just assuming it would take too long or they wouldn't be able to learn? Didn't they deserve better than that?"

Here's the thing about training: it's a double-edged sword. Unlike broader efforts like new-supervisor education or executive development programs, training equips people to do specific jobs. It allows them to specialize and become excellent in defined skill sets. During flush or even stable times, training is differentiating and potent. However, when industries or disciplines are restructured and dislocated, this same specialized training can become a shackle. It gives the employee few places to move horizontally, and it restricts the employee's ability to restart in a new industry. Furthermore, it identifies the individual with a specific industry and salary structure that in all likelihood no longer exist.

Retraining and repurposing employees is noble and desirable, but it works best in the largest companies, which are more protected from competition and where exogenous changes are slower. Leaders should also bear in mind the risk of unintended consequences in the form of entitlement attitudes. Employees may think, "Since I survived this long, I must be excellent." Or, "General-purpose soldiers are more flexible, and, besides, a loyal workforce with a long institutional memory is much more valuable than having a bunch of out-of-nowhere hotshots." Or, "My career development is the company's job, not mine. I've put in my time, and I've earned the right to be promoted."

Statements like these, whether articulated or simply taken as articles of faith, should be serious warning signs for you as a leader. A well-designed and closely monitored performance management system—one that requires every employee to define specific goals and objectives and requires every manager to hold employees accountable for achieving their objectives—can go a long way toward erasing entitlement attitudes and replacing them with a focus on results. As with most behavior-change techniques, what you reward is what people will generally make their best effort to do.

Knowing all this, and having conducted a thoughtful situational analysis of his market dynamics and the talent profile in the company, Greg made the tough decision to cast a new team. I believe that the competitive companies of the future—even those with a strong loyalty legacy—will find they need to make deliberate decisions to cast their talent pools for rapidly changing environments, looking for hunters, farmers, rock stars, and plumbers, too, if that's what it will take to win.

14

Early, Not Elegant

It's very tempting to jazz up a product or service, giving it all the bells and whistles you can think of to differentiate it in the marketplace. We see this all the time, especially with new technology. For more than a decade, software developers have been having fun programming refrigerators to do things like alert owners to an ajar door or display recipes that incorporate the ingredients inside. Most reviews of these innovative products have a decided "let's just wait and see" tone about them. Flashy technology may burnish a company's brand image, but it doesn't necessarily drive sales.

A similar phenomenon occurs in general business situations. Think about the employee who becomes so obsessed with creating a dazzling and complex PowerPoint presentation for her keynote speech that she misses every preliminary deadline, fails to share her content in advance with the conference organizer, and doesn't have time to test whether the embedded video will actually play flawlessly on the show laptop in the auditorium. By the time she takes the stage, she has already lost the goodwill of much of her audience.

It's a truism in the twenty-first century that product design and development should start with customer needs rather than technology possibilities, yet few companies seem to take that to heart. It's equally true that focusing on the core needs of customers can help solve or avoid many execution problems including quality misses, delivery delays, and disappointing installation experiences. Yet many companies still let their internal processes drive execution. Any company that can get into a new market first with high quality will enjoy a big advantage over competitors (at least until they catch up). But if you fall in love with technology complexity and let internal processes drive your metrics, the chances of holding onto that market advantage are slim.

Decision Point: Balancing Product Complexity with Market Entry

In most phases of creating a product or service, there is more than enough complexity to go around. Plenty can and does go wrong without inviting more trouble through an overly complex approach. Opting for robust, reliable, and simple is still a good choice, even in today's tech-savvy and tech-hungry market. The next story illustrates the dynamics of going simple and early to market versus taking an overly ambitious approach.

Illustrative Story

Marisa was asked to lead the development of a new next-generation platform for her company's midrange products. The corresponding assignment for the high-end platform went to Gerry. Each leader brought a different set of sensibilities to the task. One of the leaders succeeded, and one did not.

Marisa was in a good position to get started since she had just returned from an enlightening circuit of customer visits. The current generations of products were great, customers said, but they had come in a bit low in performance for new applications. What's more, every new application required a new product, and the cost of maintaining pools of spares was excessive. The customers wanted significant improvements in features and performance, as well as lower per-unit cost.

These customers aren't asking for much, Marisa thought sarcastically, *just a product that costs less for each application, delivers six times the performance, and can scale in applications and price performance for the next five years!*

Marisa set about trying to deliver what the customers wanted, within reason. She and her team came up with a modular architecture, integrated many industry-standard approaches to drive down cost structures, and chose specific areas to differentiate such as input/output, device integration, and software development. The first platform came out on schedule, with a limited feature set. It was rapidly adopted, and the market began to take notice. Clearly, the performance of the new generation of products was a significant improvement. Since most of the code used in the platform was similar to code used in other platforms, the risk inherent in developing new or untested software was minimal. Momentum grew, application by application. Over the next two years, sales doubled. The initiative was a huge success, with one win after another, speedy introduction of new features, and a heady sense of market momentum.

Now let's look at Gerry's situation. He chose to focus on the requirements of one customer that viewed itself as the most innovative in the market, figuring that visible success with this influential thought-leader would pave the way for a flood of orders. Meeting the customer's demands would require new architectures for both hardware and software. Special data structures were necessary, along with new generations of a semiconductor that was available from only one source in the world. Considering the new software, new hardware, new semiconductors, new team, and complexity of integration involved, Gerry set a delivery date that was one year later than the customer had requested. Given the delay, the customer asked for some additional features that hadn't been in the original specifications.

A vicious cycle began. Because of the new requests and the challenge of simultaneously assuring quality on all levels of invention, the development program slipped. The finished product was ultimately delivered thirty months late. When the project began, there had been no competitor in the market; thirty months later, there were two. The new competitors didn't offer as many features, but they were already absorbed into the networks of their customers and could develop new features tailored to their customers' needs. In other words, they were "sticky" to their customers. Gerry's programs became known as the most technically sophisticated in the market, but word spread that they were always late. Over time, the sales force gradually began to push Gerry's products to the bottom of their sell lists, unwilling to put their compensation at risk.

What's the moral of these two stories? First, we saw the highly positive effect of Marisa's bias for early market entry, simple devices, and learning from customers. Her products were a huge success, and the company made money. Second, we saw Gerry succeed in producing complex, technologically noteworthy products, yet fail in the marketplace because he couldn't deliver them quickly or reliably.

Trying to be all things for all comers by being endlessly willing to customize can create problems for the bottom line. So can opting for complexity simply because the company is capable of creating it. When a company is chronically late bringing a new product or service to market, competitors can jam a foot in the door and alienate your existing customer base. In general, when we have a choice, I encourage my team to go for the simpler product or service and early market entry. Simply put, "early versus overly": maintain a bias for *early* customer adoption *versus overly* risky, complex, and elegant programs.

Situational Awareness and Judgment:
Looking through the Lens

Once again, I invite you to take a step back and look at the stories in this section through the lens of courage, process, and details.

Q. Brendan dealt with two situations that required managing risk. He did very well with the first one, which was about timing the transition from an old product to a new one. He had a much harder time with the second, which involved moving manufacturing from Mexico to China. Considering the three elements of courage, process, and details, which played the most important role in Brendan's first situation? Was it also the most important element in the second situation?

Q. In your company, how are important planning teams usually put together? Who picks the team members? How is work assigned? Does energy stay high from the first meeting to the postmortem? And how is the transition back to business as usual handled when the project ends? Would Corinne's approach work in your company?

Q. Do you know what "quality" means to your customers? Does it mean the same thing to all of them?

Q. Have you ever been on a team that prioritized schedule over quality? What happened? How could you have ensured higher quality without becoming dangerously slow to market?

Q. Do you think glare in organizations is the result of a failure of courage, a lack of process, inattention to details, or something else? Can you think of a time when you simply couldn't see what was in front of you? What was getting in the way?

Q. Best-effort approaches can be energizing ... until things start to go wrong. What made Stuart and Liz decide to pull the plug on best effort and focus on managing expectations? Why do you think Liz saw it as a question of character?

Q. Does your own track record of hiring indicate that you have a bias for filling jobs from the inside versus hiring from outside? Do you know what your actual ratio has been?

Q. Have you ever hired someone out of a bias for loyalty and realized later that it would have been better to find a specialist? When you realized that, was your original hire still in the job? What did you do?

Q. If Gerry had been more situationally aware, he probably could have anticipated that the sales force would resist selling his product. Knowing what you know about Gerry, why do you think he didn't take that into account?

Part III
About Alignment

15

Demystifying Gross Margins

A company is a living creature made up of many parts working together to generate motion or inertia. For forward momentum to be sustained over the long term, all of the parts must be maintained in some kind of constructive tension with one another, even as they move around and are replaced by other parts. I say "must be maintained" because someone actively has to maintain it; the constructive tension—that alignment—won't sustain itself naturally. As most physicists will tell you, disorder in nature is generally more probable than order. When the elements fall out of sync, disharmony sets in, and forward motion stops. It's a bit like a car engine that isn't firing on all cylinders. Performance drops off, and eventually there will be a serious breakdown. In essence, ensuring that doesn't happen to a company is what alignment is about, and it's part of your job as a leader.

In Part III, we'll look at a few high-stakes business situations in which success and even survival depend on alignment. Let's start with something fundamental in any business: the alignment needed to drive favorable gross margins, which in turn drive profitability.

Understanding how to create profits is one of the most basic requirements for any business leader, but unfortunately, business schools don't spend much time on the subject. As a result, many people land in jobs with P&L responsibility but no idea how to construct plans for gross margin improvement, let alone how to execute those plans. They don't understand the mechanics that contribute to gross margin, and they often lack the leadership skills required for aligned execution across multiple functions in the company.

Actually, the basic elements driving positive gross margins are simple. In fact, we encounter them every day as consumers. Consider going to the movies with a friend. My most recent bill for a night out at the movies was $18.00 for two tickets, and $12.75 for two medium drinks and a large popcorn. To state the obvious, theaters have figured out how to get great margins on the refreshments, although the profit margins on the films are lower. Big-box retailers could sell the popcorn at a profit for less than fifty cents, and the drinks could be profitably sold at fast-food outlets for less than a dollar. The dynamic is pretty clear: once you buy the ticket and prepare for a two-hour movie (assuming that you're following the rules and not bringing your own refreshments into the theater), you become captive; the theater has a monopoly on in-house refreshments. It enjoys some other margin-related advantages, too:

- It has few competitors, and none for refreshments.
- It has many customers. If you don't buy something, the next person will, and there are many "next persons."
- It has scale and economics. As a chain, the theater may exercise buying power by choosing Coke over Pepsi, for example. The chain can buy in volume, lowering what it pays for products.
- It has complexity of value. The theater is the one-stop shop for a movie, amusement (arcade games), refreshments, and children's entertainment.
- It has speed of absorption and early delivery. In the case of a special prerelease showing, it may be the only theater within thirty miles to screen a new movie, allowing it to edge out its competitors and capitalize on the anticipation created by advertising.
- It has intellectual property. If you are the only theater in the area offering IMAX, 3-D, special showings, and such, you might command a higher ticket price.

The principles of margin, then, should be clear to most savvy moviegoers. But putting the principles into practice can be more challenging when you run your own company or are responsible for the performance of someone else's. Let's take a look at some of those challenges.

Decision Point: Finding Sustainable Value

No product or industry is blessed with inherent and permanently favorable gross margins. Gross margins are created by the fluid interplay of numerous factors including customer readiness, competitive environment, and product differentiation, as well as more obvious elements such as cost and capacity. Unless you take the time to understand the details of your specific business and industry, gross margin improvement is likely to be hit or miss. In the following story, Mike uncovers six rules of thumb that help him drive repeatable and more predictable gross margin improvement.

Illustrative Story

In his new role as general manager, Mike's job involved leading one of the hot areas in high tech during the telecom boom. But in the wake of the 2001 bust, "hot" no longer applied. He wasn't surprised to see low morale in his new team. After all, revenues had plummeted more than tenfold during the crash. As Mike studied the financials, though, he noticed some anomalies. Some items were selling at negative gross margins, and some were still fairly profitable. Since his group was responsible for many products, he would have to decide which would stay and which would go. He looked more deeply into the margin structure of his products, but the sheer number of products made it difficult to discern the business model or path to improvement. He asked for opinions.

Some members of Mike's team told him that there was just too much competition, so they expected average selling prices to decline for quite a while to come. Others said supply chain management was too weak to support the products. Admittedly, customers had complained about that as well. Mike's own research and his consultations with the team gave him plenty to think about. He preferred to deliberate long and hard before making a move, but once he had settled on a course of action, he wasn't afraid to take risks, as long as the proper planning for implementation had been done first.

For the next month, Mike studied each product line and its gross margins. He talked with customers. He kept talking with his team, too, asking questions and gathering information. The team's morale began to improve, and as theirs did, so did Mike's. Finally, he felt he had enough information to draw a few conclusions:

Conclusion 1: Speed of absorption and being early to market are a crucial bias for higher gross margins.

Said another way, when the telecom market crashed, customers were not in a rush to buy new products and services. With no sense of urgency driving buying behavior, customers told Mike's company to go away until the price got low enough. In a sense, when time to implement is infinite, everything looks like a commodity. Under these conditions, a whiteboard pitch from a competitor is as good as a working product from your company. The cycle just keeps perpetuating. On the other hand, if you pick an area where there is a high need for speed and you have product, eventually the negotiations must end and implementation must begin. When you are the first or second in a new market and the market is itching to take off at double-digit quarter-over-quarter growth rates, gross margins should be high.

Conclusion 2: Fewer competitors are a crucial bias for higher gross margins.

In one product area, Mike found a maximum of fourteen customers and roughly ten competitors. With that kind of ratio, each customer could develop extreme intimacy with one company and use another as a second source to ensure supply chain continuity. While this seemed like a favorable situation for customers, fragmentation would erect barriers to entry from one customer to another, and Mike's gross margins would suffer. However, finding product areas where there would be very few competitors would bias higher gross margins, if other biases also aligned. Watch out for competitors who do not need to make money in your product category, whether it's a startup that will operate at a loss for a protracted period or a large company that uses profit sanctuary cross subsidies to pollute profits in your niche in order to drive out competition.

Conclusion 3: Having more—rather than fewer—customers in an available market creates a bias for greater gross margins.

Mike noticed that in one area he had ten customers who wanted roughly the same thing. Only two companies could provide an appropriate device. Because Mike believed he had the best product, he could afford to walk away from a customer who was requesting irrational pricing. He figured that at worst he would be a second source, and that at best the claims of his competitors would be disproved and the customer would come back and ask for his product at a price Mike felt was fair. Mike realized that customer diversity and mix were essential areas to exploit as he began to manage the margin mix of his portfolio. As you examine your product line, look for customer diversity and try to find the perfect match between your products and the most receptive customers. If you study the products you sell and the markets you serve, you'll see patterns emerge that you can turn to your advantage, just as Mike did.

Conclusion 4: Ability to serve with differentiated scale and economics can favorably bias gross margins.

With another product, Mike had three competitors in a market of eight major consumer-brand companies. The up-front costs for this product were the highest in his portfolio, and supply chain management pressures were fierce. But Mike had twice the capacity of the rest of the industry, and the quality of what he shipped (measured as defect density) was 50 percent better than his competition. As a result, customers were willing to pay a premium for his product, both to accommodate capacity needs during seasonal spurts and to secure the higher-quality product. So Mike's higher up-front costs for this product had no negative effect on profitability and created a win-win situation for both his company and his customers.

Conclusion 5: Unique intellectual property protection and differentiation drives higher gross margins.

In two product lines, Mike discovered he had unique intellectual property that his competitors would need to license from him. This allowed him to determine (within rational envelopes) the cost basis of the industry, with some slight advantage. Where he had differentiation, gross margins were quite favorable, something he would need to keep in mind as new products came into the pipeline.

Conclusion 6: Customers will support favorable gross margins in return for significant complexity and differentiated advantage.

Mike discovered several products that took numerous older generations of product and shrank the packaging into a single package of higher reliability, lower power dissipation, and lower cost. Customers, he reasoned, should be willing to pay prices for these products that would support a very favorable new level of gross margin. If customers could reduce their costs and gain efficiency in design and procurement, why not enable improved gross margins? In this situation, packaging more functions per unit increased customer value, which was rewarded with higher gross margins.

Mike decided to test these conclusions by picking two product items and comparing their ability to extract profits. The spider chart in Figure 15.1 maps the six dimensions of gross margin bias.

Figure 15.1: Gross Margin Tensions

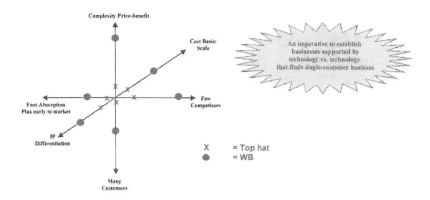

Table 1 shows the valuation mechanism used to plot the points on the spider chart.

Table 1: Product A vs. B

Axis	Score A	Score B	Comment
Speed of absorption	4	3	
Few competitors	4	1	Product A has one competitor and ten customers. Product B has three competitors and one customer.
Many customers	4	1	
Differentiated scale/process	4	1	
Unique intellectual property	3	1	
Complexity and differentiated advantage	5	1	
Actual gross margin	Greater than 45 percent	Less than 20 percent	

Looking again at Figure 15.1, the greater the area under the curve, the more likely it is that a product will achieve relatively higher gross margins.

Using this analysis, Mike brought discipline to the product selection and development process. Each product manager used it to analyze how the current market dynamics of proposed customer benefit and competitive outlook would support the business model that Mike was developing. More important, Mike was able to use this tool to explode the many myths he had encountered as his team rationalized why their gross margins were not up to expectations. This was useful in turning product managers who felt like victims into product managers who made deliberate decisions and hunted for improved margins. The methodology also pointed to areas where internal investments needed to be made. On some product lines, Mike would invest in process differentiation. On others, investment would go into new product development that miniaturized more functions.

Mike looked forward to the day when the markets he served would once again become innovation driven. When that happened, time would again become an important criterion. He remembered some lessons other executives had taught him:

- Get big, get niched, or get out.
- You need to achieve 20 percent market share to be profitable.
- In a rapidly growing market, gross margins should improve between half a percentage point and 2 percent for each point of market share you have above 20 or 30 percent, depending on the markets and other factors.

With these tenets in mind, Mike set out to redefine the product portfolio and mix of the business he was charged to manage. He would seek markets and products likely to bring great gross margins. Just as important, he would need to balance multiple factors to maintain alignment and hold on to those gross margins. For example, if uniqueness in intellectual property eroded over time, he might have to ensure manufacturing scale and economics that would enable sustained margins. These alignment adjustments would spark intense conversations for Mike and his engineers and product managers in the months ahead.

Clearly, it is easier to hypothesize a gross margin structure than it is to achieve one, and it is easier to achieve a structure than it is to maintain that structure as markets slow down and competition grows. As we saw in this story, delivering excellent product gross margins requires:

- *courage* to make choices in products with specific profits;
- a *process* to examine and drive a discipline of execution along differentiating lines; and
- recognition that value comes from getting the *details* right.

16

On Post-M&A Integration

Most managers aren't called upon to make go or no-go decisions about mergers and acquisitions, but they do play important roles in the integration phase. They are responsible for ensuring that the company is properly aligned after the deal goes through; failure to do so can undermine the market advantages the merger or acquisition was intended to provide. Having been instrumental in more than one hundred M&A transactions and integrations in the high-tech world, I know that the reality of such activity is anything but glamorous. Financial success is fleeting, and the leader's daily experience is defined by interactions with employees who are typically disappointed and left without direction. By the time the ink has dried on the closing documents, employees are also pretty well disgusted by the executives in charge of the transaction, whose celebratory grip-and-grin publicity photos have been replaced by confusing project management spreadsheets generated during late-night meetings and heavily populated with blank spaces and question marks.

When mergers and acquisitions are viewed solely as financial or asset transactions, it's hard to extract the best practices most likely to lead to success. Volumes have been written on this topic, and I won't pretend in this brief chapter to distill the collective wisdom about how or when to do a deal. Instead, this chapter tells the story of two high-tech paths. One emphasized small acquisitions. The other took the form of a series of mergers. One path, while not perfect, was successful. The other was inherently less successful and in fact led to years of corporate rehabilitation.

> ### Decision Point: Accomplishing Cultural Integration Post M&A
>
> Even when employees are excited about a merger or acquisition and are determined to make it work, harmonizing disparate company cultures will never happen on its own. Without aggressive intervention from leadership, the entities will devolve into inert, resistant tribes. Acquisitions (especially those disingenuously described as "mergers of equals") rarely succeed unless leaders take overt action to proclaim, define, role model, and reward new cultural identifications and behaviors. The new organization must recruit all employees into the future.

Two Illustrative Stories

Steve's company had become excellent at acquisitions. It focused on acquiring businesses that were young, and it had a history of introducing products early in new markets. The acquisition targets employed fifty to one hundred people, two-thirds of whom were engineers. There were typically around ten sales leads and a dozen or two corporate staffers. In general, the companies were too young to have built up large manufacturing organizations or large sales forces. By the time a deal closed, the engineers on both sides of the transaction were engaged and impressed by one another's capabilities, and they had developed a road map of common product that they considered formidable against the competition. Both sides shared a common view of the "why" of the acquisition, which was less about the current generation of product than about the next generation and the team of engineers who would make it.

The discipline of integration had become just that, a discipline. Alignment was caused, not taken for granted. Steve created a central integration team to manage the process, and on the day the deal closed, all the acquired employees knew their benefits, their new boss, and their assignments. The new management team had already actively recruited each employee into his or her new role, clearly describing the corporate culture they would all be part of. Senior leaders from the acquired company were likewise recruited, often as early as during the due diligence process, in the hope that they would bring new ideas and insight to the going-forward company. Because Steve's company was many times bigger than the companies it acquired, the integration model was clear: the smaller target would be assimilated into the larger company's processes, buildings, parking spaces, social norms, and so on; it was an experience of total consumption, dominated by the acquiring organism. The company's post-acquisition success rate was the highest in its peer group, due in large part to precise talent selection and recruitment, and disciplined integration processes.

Halfway across the country from Steve, Karin was having a harder time. A leader in her company, she had learned firsthand that M&A activity can cause major headaches. After a long cycle of mergers, her company had become quite large, and she had a hard time describing who or what the company was anymore. Even several years after the merger frenzy had slowed, there was no single corporate culture. At least three different groups in three different cities thought that where they worked was the company headquarters. Each group referred to the others either by location ("the Santa Barbara people") or by function ("the development people"), but never by their names or the names of their leaders.

Even though common analytical systems, including Oracle and Essbase, had been deployed, employees ignored them and continued to use Excel spreadsheets to manage numbers, complaining all the while about the unavailability or unreliability of company-wide financial projections. In one case, Karin drove for two hours to visit a remotely located finance leader. When she got to his office, she sat in his chair and proceeded to strip Excel from his laptop. He found that outrageous, which it probably was, but Karin was desperate. She viewed her action as one small step toward forcing alignment and improving the company.

Meanwhile, in Santa Barbara, morale was abysmal. The developers complained constantly that they were victims of circumstance. Everything had gone down the drain, they said, when San Jose replaced Santa Barbara as the headquarters location. They were convinced that the product managers in San Jose were vapid. One day at an informal skip-level breakfast, Karin asked the Santa Barbara team if they were happy with the way things were going. They all said no, and that things had been so much better before all the mergers. She asked if they had a plan to improve morale. The team said no, it didn't, and there wasn't anything they could do about it anyway, since they were at the mercy of the San Jose product managers, who got their power from political connections rather than competence.

Karin sat still and silently counted to five, trying to control her exasperation. She asked if the Santa Barbara developers knew the names of the San Jose product managers. They said they did. She delivered a brief lecture on teamwork and pointed out that people with a sincere team orientation usually refer to one another by name, not by geography or function. She then asked the developers when they had last discussed requirements directly with customers. "Never," they said emphatically. "So, let me understand," Karin said. "You think the product managers who ask you to build things are stupid, but you build whatever they ask and never talk to a customer yourselves?" Blank looks were the only answer.

Even five years after the fact, this post-merger team still yearned to live in the past. They thought and behaved like victims, and their attitude was contagious. This phenomenon is extremely common. In fact, negative attitudes can take root even if the premerger environment was unpleasant to work in and financially unsuccessful. In the hazy light of invented nostalgia, the past is always better than the present, even when it was actually much worse.

Steve and Karin's experiences suggest some common insights:

- Any merger or acquisition is the result of an overt choice on the part of the leaders. The majority of employees have nothing to say about it. If you want to achieve true integration and alignment, there must be a dominant surviving culture, and each retained employee must essentially be recruited and invited to make an overt choice to be part of the new asset.
- People are habitual. If you want them to believe that things are different, change their parking spaces, their buildings, or the food in the cafeteria. Redecorate the lobby. Otherwise they'll show up at work and act the same way they have for years—like victims ready to blame other employees for their mistakes. Change the parking spaces!
- By their nature, processes memorialize and preserve the past. They carry instructions, lexicons, codified organizational interactions, and expectations that were defined in the past, based on past circumstances. If you want to integrate effectively, homogenize the respective company processes

and normalize them quickly. You'll end up doing it eventually, and the longer you wait, the messier it will be. As the old saying goes, "Pay now or pay later." It's much better to pay now. What's more, this sends a clear signal to employees that the company is moving forward and they need to let go of the past.

- Be prepared to move people out and bring new people in. Possibly as many as one-third to one-half of the current employees will meet your rerecruiting efforts with inertia. The surviving company deserves an employee base that wants the new asset to succeed. You may need to remove those people who drift along for the ride and never make an overt choice to embrace the new.

These four organizational insights hold true for small acquisitions as well as larger mergers. However, managers tend to face more impedance in the larger mergers, a function of their greater complexity and the existence of more moving parts. The situations are very different, but they share similar remedies.

As a leader, you may not be happy about a merger or acquisition, and there's no doubt that they disrupt operations and can emotionally rattle employees, from the lowest levels in the organization to the highest. But mergers and acquisitions are a fact of corporate life and sometimes even a necessary condition for survival. You can help your company move through the process more successfully if you remember and respect the power of the human factor in organizations.

Specifically, you should take some of these steps: Recruit all talent overtly and explicitly. Make some visible, symbolic changes in the environment to signal a new start. Don't tolerate tribalism, retreats to zones of safety, or "us versus them" thinking. (This requires *courage*!) Integrate disparate systems and practices as quickly and thoroughly as you reasonably can. (Integration is a *process*!) Finally, think of M&A as an opportunity, not only for your company, but for you personally. I can look around my company today and identify many individuals whose reputations and responsibilities grew significantly as a direct result of the way they led their teams through an M&A experience and into a new world of possibilities. (The way someone leads through the *details* of integration truly makes a difference!)

17

Working with the Board

Seen from the outside, boards of directors are something of a mystery. Only when there's a headline-making organizational coup, corporate scandal, or shareholder agitation do the workings of a board become exposed, usually in a highly dramatic and emotionally charged way.

Boards that run smoothly tend to be quietly effective, doing their jobs behind the scenes, supporting and challenging company leadership, and enabling responsible company performance.

As a result, most managers get very little opportunity to watch the normal operations of boards of directors. They have no way to prepare themselves for the day when they will be called upon to interact with and influence them. When that day comes, these managers tend to approach the first board meeting as if they were entering a forbidden and vaguely hostile fortress. They are usually anxious, overprepared, and focused on making their points (and a good impression) rather than on listening and engaging.

Like the other teams described in this book, boards of directors are collections of individuals. Each member has his or her own personality, agenda, and perspective. For example, a passionate believer in the value of shareholder dividends may advocate for them regardless of the company's financial situation or position in the market. Board members, too, may be tourists, gatherers, or collectors. The tourists enjoy occupying board seats but are ill prepared to put themselves on the line when circumstances call for courage. The gatherers listen carefully and sample the views expressed. They absorb the conversations, but they don't take the next step of filtering out the noise so they can focus on the critical few issues facing the board at that specific moment in time. The collectors do take that important step, distilling valuable information and developing relevant insights so they can bring value to their roles on behalf of the company and its shareholders.

I have served on thirteen boards and chaired one, so I've had plenty of time to observe them in action. I'm convinced that the key to working successfully with a board is gaining and maintaining alignment—that is, creating a smooth and predictable cadence of ongoing communication between the board and management. While interaction with the board of directors may lie in the future for some readers, the best practices in this chapter may help you support your executives in their board relationships today and prepare you for your own executive responsibilities when that day comes. I hope it also demonstrates that the leadership principles we've been exploring throughout this book are relevant from the factory floor to the boardroom.

Decision Point: Maintaining Alignment by Understanding Roles

The role of a company's board of directors should never be mysterious. Much disruptive drama and finger-pointing could be prevented if senior leaders, rank-and-file employees, investors, and members of the media understood what the board should and should not be held accountable for. The following discussion is my attempt to build that understanding.

The Board's Job

First, contrary to popular belief, boards don't (or shouldn't) actually *manage* anything in the company. They essentially serve as representatives of the shareholders. As such, they have a fairly clear and precise agenda built around seven things:

1. They hire and fire the CEO. In addition, they should ensure the continuity and level of talent of the management team by holding the executive and human resources teams accountable for succession planning.
2. They make sure the company has a strategy with an adequate business model. Put very simply, they must have reason to believe that the management team knows how to make money.
3. They insist upon and should model tone at the top when it comes to ethics and integrity. Ultimately, the buck stops with the board, though it hits the CEO's desk first.
4. They keep an eye on resource allocation to make sure the company has a process for ensuring that resources are being used to maximum benefit.
5. They monitor metrics to be sure the company is measuring the right things.
6. They arbitrate risks. Ultimately, it is the board that decides how much risk the company should be willing to take.
7. They oversee the use of cash in the business; this includes decisions about mergers and acquisitions, stock buybacks and dividends, the company's overall capital structure, and how much should be given back, and in what form, to the shareholders.

Seven things, not seventy, and they're all matters of governance, not matters of (or for) management. Unfortunately, most board members aren't aligned on their own role, which means they can't be aligned with management on who should be doing what. That's a recipe for friction. My guess is that for one-third of all boards, it takes a company crisis to get the members focused on those seven responsibilities. Another third never will. So the management team—whose day-to-day job, after all, is solving problems—steps in to fill the void and is met with hostility from board members who thinks the CEO is overstepping. Deadlock!

So the first step in gaining alignment between management and the board is cognitive: establishing a shared understanding of the role each group will play in the life of the company. The second step, which we'll cover next, is behavioral, specifically, communicating and influencing.

Interacting Successfully

Even though the full board may meet formally only once every quarter, five simple communication practices can go a long way toward building your confidence and their confidence in you.

- Hold a pre-board meeting or executive session immediately before every quarterly meeting. Provide a synopsis of the issue at hand or the company's recent performance. Invite questions and comments, and listen closely for areas of disagreement that might surface in the larger session.
- Conduct midquarter calls every six weeks to keep the board from feeling that you are disconnected or distracted. These calls keep you engaged in the way the board members are thinking and will help you shape meeting material so that it is responsive to board concerns.
- Invite and incorporate board members' feedback in developing agendas for the board meetings.
- Provide a written executive summary at least once per quarter, preferably one or two weeks before the regular board meeting. This is an opportunity to distill and clarify performance issues, highlight progress and challenges, and establish a tone of transparency and candor.

- Involve board members by asking for advice and support in advancing your agenda.

The art of influencing is more difficult to codify, and it starts with understanding who the board members are, how they behave individually, and how they are likely to behave as a group. By definition, individuals who are selected to serve on boards are generally bright people. They come from different industries and have lived through different experiences, all of which informs their perceptions and assumptions. They all have egos and agendas; that doesn't make them selfish people, but it does make them people with specific points of view. A CEO must bridge the board agenda, individual points of view, and the realities of the company.

Here is an illustration taken from actual events on the board of a high-tech company. This company had gone through cataclysmic industry contraction over several decades. Where there once had been some four hundred companies, only four survived (eventually, that shrunk to two). Three previous CEOs were on the board, and they decided they needed a visionary to balance the old guard. They found such a person and brought him in. Over time, they added more new blood. Instead of becoming revitalized, though, the board almost immediately became polarized. Voting blocs formed, and every decision became a choice between new and old. Nothing got done.

Why were so many bright people so ineffective? It was because their agendas were fundamentally different. The legacy board members were protecting their view of the past. The new board members were pushing for change. While there were lengthy and colorful conversations about individuals, there were no conversations about the most basic issue: how to reconcile and align the two agendas.

A physicist considering this situation might see it this way: With ego and stature comes a high degree of potential energy, that is, capability without motion or promise, not producing outcomes. That is not the ideal state for a board of directors. Ideally, boards are sources of directed kinetic energy. If you're the CEO, the best way to control and convert potential energy is to force relationships one at a time, getting to know board members and aligning them with your agenda. Otherwise, entropy takes over. Entropy, popularly understood as a tendency toward disorder, can take many forms. In a board situation, it may be the same question getting asked over and over again without any progress or resolution. Once entropy sets in, the best possible result is stasis; the worst is chaos.

As you go about connecting with board members individually and over a period of time, you will notice that most of them have a signature personal agenda or propensity that comes out in just about every meeting. For example, some are convinced that the only way to compensate company executives is to rate them on a relative scale of total shareholder return or return on invested capital, independent of whether the company is a turnaround candidate, a momentum player, or a steady franchise. These people are philosophical zealots on their particular subject and will advocate for it in every meeting they attend and with every board on which they serve.

They don't do this out of malice or ineptitude, by the way. People have a strong desire to be relevant. For board members who are not day-to-day working executives—who may be retired, for example—the board is the stage on which they can demonstrate their relevance. It's not difficult to see how fixations or even stridency might be the result. Creating one-on-one relationships that allow each board member to feel heard and respected can go a long way in keeping stridency out of board proceedings.

Many CEOs assume that "people are people" and make the mistake of attempting to manage their board the same way they manage the teams in their company. That won't work. Boards are not high-performance teams, nor are they intended to be. They are governance bodies composed of individuals. If the CEO is diligent about maintaining communication and influencing members one by one, the CEO and the board are likely to remain productively aligned.

18

The Fish and the Mailman

You're serious about being the best leader you can be. You think. You plan. You ask for coaching. You read books like this … But let's face it: things are going to go wrong. Let's take a look at four communications technology projects and their four talented development managers. All the projects began at about the same time, but they ended in very different ways.

Decision Point: Ensuring Repeatable Results

It's tempting for leaders—especially those who are seen as up-and-coming superstars—to let the force of their personalities influence their approach to business challenges. But while those leaders often make an initial splash, they tend to lose their way. The most successful leaders are able to set force of personality aside and focus instead on meticulous planning, ongoing communication with customers, disciplined risk management, and team alignment. As a result, they enjoy the rewards that come with a succession of roles and opportunities, and when they leave companies, it's by their choice and on their terms. Predictability matters!

Illustrative Story

Don was smart and knew it. In fact, he thought he could develop software faster than anybody else. Because of his reputation, he figured he could hire top talent away from anyone and give them free rein to exercise their creative flair. Don's latest project was software development for a new directory server that would integrate names, addresses, and the provisioning and terms and conditions of services. He was excited by the aggressive timeline for his project.

Jo prided herself on building what other people could not. She liked hard problems with elegant solutions, and she brought in people who could envision the future and build things that would still be relevant ten years out. Jo began a new switch development that would replace the call control fabric of the telephone network. This was an exciting next-generation architecture that would be sure to attract top talent inside and outside the company.

Tony was a different kind of individual altogether. He loved beginnings and knew how to whip up excitement about a new project.

He saw no reason to put a detailed plan in place before jumping into action; in fact, he believed that would just slow things down. With his high-energy, high-confidence approach, he easily attracted people to his projects and had earned a reputation as an aggressive and charismatic manager. Tony began development of a new security server. It was a top priority, and he was pretty sure he could cobble together some old pieces of technology and get prototypes out quickly. No need to make a detailed plan yet, he decided.

Last, but not least, Ed was a seasoned developer. Much like the master woodworker who measures twice and cuts once, Ed enjoyed a good challenge, but he also believed in deliberate planning and precise execution. Ed was asked to develop a product that would transmit voice-over-data links. Several industry experts believed this would be technically impossible to do well since voice requires very low latency. In other words, there couldn't be pauses in the transmission and continuity of the voice because distortion would result. But the challenge excited Ed, who felt that the skills his team had developed working on a prior project might be applicable.

All four projects started out with a bang, but it wasn't long before three of them were in jeopardy. Don's team beat their deadline for delivering beta software to the customer, but the rate of new bugs or errors found in system tests was increasing, and the severity of the problems also trended up. After a year of development, Don compared the plan to the actual results and saw that from a resource perspective the team was 25 percent off the initial plan (see Figure 18.1). The engineers were demoralized because it seemed they would never get the quality required for general availability. The company's executive team was distressed because the sales force and customers had been promised a product, but no one really knew when that product would be available. The CEO could see from the charts below that money was being sucked into a vortex of no return, and serious decisions would need to be made soon.

Figure 18.1: Don's Plan versus Actual Scorecard

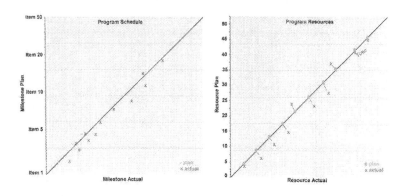

Jo had a similar problem. Her new switch development was clearly revolutionary, but although the basic software functions seemed to be in place, performance was two orders of magnitude lower than that of the current generation of products. What's more, there were fundamental architectural questions about the efficacy of the design. After a year of customer system tests and disappointing results, it was clear that the program required a reset. The architecture was elegant, but the team had missed every milestone. As each deadline came and went, Jo added new members to the team, so at the one-year mark, the team was twice as big as it had been in the beginning. The management team was now extremely concerned, and Jo's reputation was on the line.

Tony's project was also in distress. Initially, he had successfully attracted a large number of developers and captured the interest of most of the management team. But he still had no plan for turning the prototype into a product. Company expectations were high, and Tony was under pressure to give the prototype to customers. Although he didn't tell his management, he knew the security server would crumble under real-world conditions. There simply wasn't time for laborious team discussions and cross-functional validation, so Tony and two other leaders camped out in the office for thirty-six straight hours and assembled a development plan. The slap-dash road map and lack of team buy-in took a heavy toll: milestones were missed; the best engineers asked to be excused from the project; and users who were initially enthusiastic about the prototype lost confidence that the team could deliver what it promised.

Ed took a different approach. He began by assembling a small team of architects, and together they made a short list of key decisions. First, they decided to focus on a single specific application, voice transmission to small branch offices of banks. They aligned on two signature features for their product: high voice quality and lower cost. Finally, they decided to build this software on top of an existing hardware product and as an enhancement to existing software. That gave them clear focus as well as an early-entry vehicle to market via stable and characterized hardware. The plan was developed in detail with the help of an extended team of engineers who would potentially work on the product at a later date. One year later, all milestones were on track, and the project was only 10 percent over budget (see Figure 18.2). The quality of the product in the system test was excellent, and the first three customers were asking for standard product and a next release of the software that would transmit fax traffic as well as voice.

Figure 18.2: Ed's Plan versus Actual Status

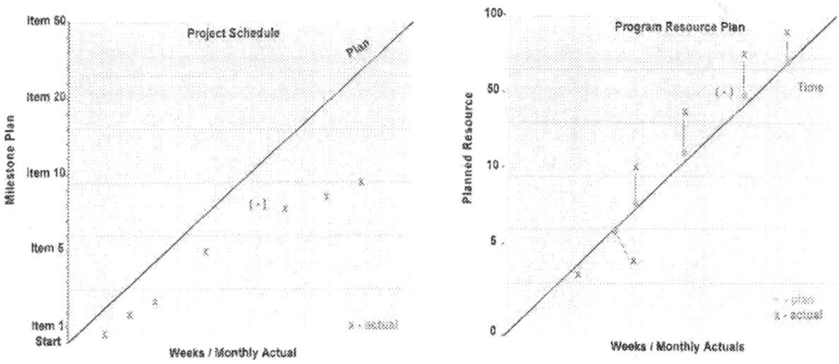

Don's, Jo's and Tony's projects ran into trouble for different reasons: low quality, too much elegance, lack of planning. To borrow an acronym from the accounting world, programs like these are **FISH: First In** the funnel as new starts, but **Still Here** because they never finish. FISH programs develop a pungent stink within an organization, and like dead fish, they ultimately pollute everything around them.

Ed understood the technical complexity of his project and assumed that things would go wrong, so he meticulously planned ahead. The sales force and customers enthusiastically embraced his product. The product worked as promised, and Ed's team delivered release after release on schedule and with high quality. He earned the trust of constituents, and trust built momentum. Metaphorically speaking, you could say that Ed was a mailman who always delivered what he promised. His team was dependable. You could set your clock by his commitments, and customers trusted their businesses to Ed's team. In the end, despite the difficulty of the voice-over-data challenge, Ed kept his work simple, planned it in detail, and managed quality and schedule every day, removing risks one at a time. Ultimately, the mailman delivered, and the fish just smelled.

There will be times when unforeseen problems (or problems you should have foreseen) send your best leadership resolutions flying out the window. The people around you will take their cues from your behavior; if you respond thoughtfully and unemotionally, and if you make it clear that you won't tolerate drama or blame, your team is more likely to stay grounded and get through the crisis with minimal collateral damage.

Generally, leaders who have the *courage* to confront issues early, employ a disciplined *process* to execute on schedule week by week, and manage the *details* of planning and execution will deliver predictably and minimize misses.

About Alignment:
Looking through the Lens

One final time, let's see whether the lens of courage, process, and details brings the chapters in this section into sharper focus.

Q. Mike's painstaking analysis of the details and his willingness to spend many weeks gathering data helped him optimize his portfolio in favor of great gross margins. Do you think anyone asked why the process was taking so long? How do you think Mike might have answered?

Q. How did Steve and Karin deliberately cause alignment in their post-M&A environments? Couldn't they have let integration happen naturally over time?

Q. Can you think of companies whose boards and leadership teams were not well aligned and became newsworthy? In your own job, how do you stay aligned with your constituents? Do you have an agreed-upon process? Is there a shared expectation for a specific level of detail, transparency, and so forth?

Q. In chapter 18, Ed was successful where Don, Jo, and Tony failed. Did courage play any part in his success, or was it all about process and details?

Conclusion

I hope you used the illustrative stories throughout this book as practice sessions, opportunities to put yourself in the scene and test what can happen in real-life situations. In some, leaders clung to superficial conventional wisdom and got trapped in "all good or all bad" polarities. In others, leaders were able to let conventional wisdom go and engage in unemotional and relentless inspections of relevant details. As we saw, one path was far more likely than the other to generate alignment and encourage sustainable positive results.

Let's recall the two fundamental beliefs I discussed in the beginning of this book:

- Organizations are organisms. They have personalities, cultures, and unwitting behaviors. While we as individuals are complex, the organizations we work in are far more so. An individual has one head and one body, while an organization comprises numerous minds and bodies. In the end, it is the *alignment* of this multithreaded structure that allows complexity to be tamed to advantage. Without alignment, complexity will eventually overwhelm the structure itself.
- Each of us views the world from the prison of our own perspectives. We see through a lens that magnifies our personal beliefs, and we tend to act in ways that are extrapolations of past experiences in which we may have succeeded or failed. In reality, leadership is tested and

learned daily by navigating situations, and the most effective leadership development is behavioral.

With those two fundamentals as the jumping-off point, we explored a variety of leadership situations. Here are the key concepts presented in each chapter:

1. People are hardwired for drama and conditioned to oversimplify. It's the job of leaders—especially leaders of public companies—to counteract these forces by exerting the force of purpose and insight. Their efforts must be conscious and visible.

2. While many organizations are glutted with professionals who act like tourists, more wisdom is to be found in the smaller group: the insightful collectors. Gatherers can be useful or counterproductive, depending in part on how skillfully a leader directs them.

3. On any given day in most organizations, you will see people who thrive on conspicuously attacking the issue of the moment. The sight is reminiscent of peewee soccer players clustered around the ball, flailing wildly while leaving the rest of the field unattended. The leader's job is to establish a well-defined process and provide opportunities for disciplined organization and practice. This way everyone learns to play his or her position.

4. When a team is chronically underperforming, check the output and ask the team what they think would help. More times than not, those who see themselves as victims will say they're overworked. A more detailed analysis, though, usually shows that improving quality and attention to the details will free people to do more new things. You can't prescribe the right remedy unless you have the right diagnosis.

5. While the temptation may be strong to hire people who are just good enough to hit the ground running, the most effective leaders hire great people one at a time, even if it takes a little longer. Every hire counts, and a few great people are superior to a bunch of good ones!

6. All too often, functional groups construct a xenophobic tribal identity that keeps them in a loose confederation relationship

with the rest of the organization. This is especially true after a merger or acquisition. To create high-functioning teams, leaders must overtly recruit each employee into the larger organization and, when necessary, hire new leaders capable of breaking down the walls of tribalism.

7. When managing product transitions, people usually understand both the beginning state and the end state but rarely how to get from one to the other. The art of leadership is in managing the speed of the transition and the art of placing the risk on your competitor. A team's ability to control the path and outcome of a transition should determine how fast it moves.

8. Risk is inevitable and can be positive if managed well. The most skillful risk managers combine good contingency planning with the kind of situational awareness cultivated in military environments.

9. Shrewd planning is a specific skill, and not everyone has it. You need it on your team, though, because executing according to a carefully constructed plan is a kind of insurance policy against managing by reacting.

10. Any debate about schedule versus quality is a lose-lose conversation. You can only move as fast as you can manage expectations. The most successful approaches start with disciplined quality processes and include aggressively managed, customer-specific expectations.

11. When an organization fails to act effectively on a known issue, the reason is usually glare, or accepted misalignment. You can lead the team out of a glare situation by focusing intensely on the facts and removing any ambiguity about accountability. Often appointing a single accountable individual—"one throat to choke"—is enough to solve the problem.

12. Best-effort organizational practices tend to neglect risk identification and remediation, making it impossible to manage customer expectations predictably. Instead, start by managing customer expectations and defining both best-case and risk-adjusted outcomes.

13. Leaders today must navigate a dilemma in workforce management: to staff based on loyalty or to staff as if casting a feature film. In highly competitive and fast-changing

environments, a loyalty-based strategy driven by successive repurposing of talent often produces mediocrity. To maximize success in competitive markets, deliberately cast your workforce for the environment and the specializations required.

14. When introducing a new product, seek out early customer feedback on whether you should develop a high-quality and functionally sufficient product, or opt for elegance despite its inherent time-based risks. Early, not elegant, is almost always the right answer.

15. Great gross margins are not always easy to find, and they are harder to hold on to. But there are six factors that, if orchestrated thoughtfully, will help you demystify the challenge.

16. When a workforce is reconstituted, whether through mergers and acquisitions or simply a large number of new hires, maintaining a common culture requires that each employee make an overt choice to be a part of the company. Unless employees explicitly adopt the attitude that they are dedicated to the furtherance of the company's objectives, they will feel and act like victims, ultimately undermining the promise of the new organization.

17. When working with the board of directors, ensure that roles are clear and universally understood, and communicate frequently to maintain alignment.

18. Managers who simplify work, mitigate risks, manage quality and schedules every day, and deliver to expectation build the trust of others. These are the mailmen who deliver. Managers who are victims of poor planning, poor quality control, overly complex architectures, and constant delays are more like fishmongers, managing projects that are first in and still here, or those that never finish.

These concepts can give you a leadership advantage, but the difference between a breakthrough leader and a highly competent one often comes down to courage. It takes courage to fully scope the dimensions of your challenge, avoiding blind spots caused by glare and reliance on conventional wisdom. For example, you may discover that you have good leaders but not domain specialists (by "domain specialist," I mean someone who has been a recognized subject matter expert in his/her field or product area for ten to twenty years,) a culture that discourages risk-taking, fast time to market but poor quality, lack of listening, and so on. Once the challenge has been fully scoped, you can design processes that will mobilize your team's energy, remediate the right things, and help you discover what you do not know. Don't underestimate that last one. (After all, if the solution could be found in what you already know, you'd probably already have found it, right?) The most significant details usually hide within the realm of what you do not know, and they often determine who wins and who loses in a marketplace battle.

As I said at the outset, the goal of this book is not to convince you to adopt this particular set of precepts, though I hope you find at least some of them useful and worth adopting. My greatest hope for this book is that it will inspire you to test, examine, and embrace your own beliefs and insights. In the end, the key to understanding your challenges—the elusive "devil"—is hiding in the details.

May you have the *courage* to challenge conventional wisdom as you strengthen your leadership and inspire others to strengthen theirs. When in doubt, *process* can be your friend. And remind yourself every day: *Details* matter!

About the Author

Dr. Kevin J. Kennedy is the coauthor of *Going the Distance: Why Some Companies Dominate and Others Fail* (Financial Times Press/Prentice Hall). He is currently the president and chief executive officer of Avaya, a global provider of business collaboration and communications solutions. He has spent much of his career in leadership positions in technology and communications companies, serving as president and chief executive officer of JDS Uniphase Corporation, as chief operating officer of Openwave Systems, and as senior vice president of the Service Provider line of business and Software Technologies division at Cisco Systems. Earlier in his career, he spent seventeen years with AT&T Bell Laboratories.

Dr. Kennedy holds a bachelor of sciences degree in engineering from Lehigh University in Pennsylvania, and master's and doctorate degrees in engineering from Rutgers University in New Jersey. In January 2011, President Barack Obama appointed him to serve on the National Security Telecommunications Advisory Committee. In the past, he was a congressional fellow to the US House of Representatives Committee on Science, Space, and Technology.

Dr. Kennedy currently serves on the boards of directors of KLA-Tencor Corporation and Digital Realty Trust, L.P.